CW00544744

LUCIANO BERIO:

TWO INTERVIEWS

Photo by Phillipe Gras

LUCIANO BERIO

TWO INTERVIEWS

with Rossana Dalmonte and Bálint András Varga

translated and edited by David Osmond-Smith

MARION BOYARS

NEW YORK . LONDON

First published in the United States and Great Britain in 1985 by

MARION BOYARS PUBLISHERS
262 West 22nd Street, New York, N.Y. 10011
24 Lacy Road, London SW15 1NL

Distributed in the United States by
The Scribner Book Companies Inc

Distributed in Canada by
John Wiley & Sons Canada Ltd.

Rossana Dalmonte's interviews originally published by
Gius. Laterza I Figli Spa, Rome-Bari, under the title
Intervista sulla musica (1981)
© Laterza, 1981

Bálint András Varga's interviews originally published by
Editio Musica, Budapest, under the title
Beszélgetések Luciano Berióval (1981)
© Bálint András Varga, 1981

© This English version Marion Boyars Publishers, 1985

Library of Congress Cataloging in Publication Data
Berio, Luciano, 1925—
    Two interviews.

    1. Berio, Luciano, 1925—.   2. Music—Addresses,
essays, lectures.   3. Composers—Italy—Interviews.
I. Dalmonte, Rossana.   II. Varga, Bálint András.
III. Bero, Luciano, 1925—.   Beszélgetések Luciano
Berióval. 1984   IV. Title.
ML60.B468413   1984   780   84-12346

British Library Cataloguing in Publication Data
Berio, Luciano
    Luciano Berio: two interviews.
    1. Music
    I. Title   II. Dalmonte, Rossana
    III. Varga, Bálint Andreas
    780'.92'4   ML160

    ISBN 0-7145-2829-3 cloth

Typeset in 11 point Baskerville by Essex Photo Set, Rayleigh.
Printed and bound in the United States of America

This book is dedicated by Luciano Berio

to Rivi and Yossi Packer

CONTENTS

Interviews with Rossana Dalmonte

Defining and discussing music – different approaches to music –
Adorno and marxist musical criticism – music and the non-
specialist – other writers on music (Boulez, Mila) – music and the
media – the baroque revival in Italy – synthesizers and their
limitations.

Berio's family background – early musical and literary experi-
ences – Puccini and *La Bohème* – studies at the Milan
Conservatorio: Ghedini – friendship with Bruno Maderna –
Dallapiccola – music in America.

Darmstadt – *Nones* and *Allelujah II* – Berio's view of serialism –
holistic musical thought: Beethoven – the separation of parameters – the fetichizing of music's raw materials.

PREFACE

In 1980-81 Luciano Berio gave two extensive interviews – the first to the Italian musicologist and critic Rossana Dalmonte, the second to the Hungarian writer Bálint András Varga. In part they had different aims. The interview with Dalmonte formed part of a series, published in Italy by Laterza, in which the nature and problems of a particular field were discussed by a representative expert, whereas the interview with Varga, published by Editio Musica, Budapest, focussed more exclusively upon Berio's life and works. Nevertheless, there were considerable overlaps between the two – as was to be expected, since Varga's interview often touched upon areas discussed by Berio with Dalmonte.

In bringing them together for English publication, it therefore seemed sensible to provide a compressed version of Dalmonte's interview, omitting those sections which are relevant only in an Italian context, and to follow it with the complementary sections from Varga's interview – notably his extended survey of Berio's vocal and theatrical works. The reader will notice a stylistic disjunction between the two. Dalmonte's interview was conducted in Italian, and subsequently revised by Berio to produce a polished, at times almost a 'literary' text. Varga's interview was conducted in English – and fluently as both he and Berio speak the language, the resultant style inevitably differs from that of native Italian translated into English. Beyond emending certain linguistic idiosyncracies in Varga's text, and pruning some of the more florid moments in Dalmonte's, I have not attempted to reconcile the two styles.

I must thank Luciano Berio warmly for making time, in the midst of a complex schedule, to read through and suggest a substantial number of alterations and additions to the English version of these interviews. But I must also thank his wife, Talia Packer Berio, the translator of the Hebrew version of Dalmonte's interview, for advance warning of many of the problems involved, Andrew Matheson for help in preparing the text of sections two and three of Dalmonte's interview, and Angela Oxley and Jane South for much patient typing.

David Osmond-Smith.

LIST OF ILLUSTRATIONS

1. Berio at Oneglia.
2. Cathy Berberian with Dallapiccola.
3. Pousseur with Berio.
4. Berio's notes on *Nones*.
5. Maderna's analysis of *Nones*.
6. Berio with Boulez.
7. Eco and Berio at Stefano Eco's christening.
8. Rehearsals for *Sinfonia*.
9. A sketch for *O King*.
10. Berio and Cathy Berberian perform *Folk Songs*.
11. Berio and Maderna.
12. A page from *A-Ronne*.
13. Berio and Sanguineti at the recording of *A-Ronne*.
14. Berio with 4X.

SOURCES OF ILLUSTRATIONS

Illustrations Nos. 2, 3, and 6 are reproduced from Musicacittà, published by Laterza for the Maggio Musicale Fiorentino, 1984. Nos. 1, 8a, 8b, 10, 13a, 13b and 14 come from Luciano Berio's own collection of photographs. No. 11 is by courtesy of Gisela Bauknecht. No. 7 is by courtesy of Renata Eco. Nos. 4a, 4b and 5 are from Luciano Berio's collection of manuscripts. No. 9 is from the editor's collection. No. 12 is by courtesy of Universal Editions, Vienna.

INTERVIEW 1

with Rossana Dalmonte

*Dalmonte: Since we are going to be talking primarily about music, I think
we ought to start by sorting out what you understand music to be.*

Berio: I'm tempted to reply that music is the art of sounds, but
then you'll ask me what art is, which would be worse still. I'm
afraid I can't give you an answer. It's a difficult question, and in
some ways rather an indiscreet one too. Difficult because for
producers and receivers alike (if that's a valid distinction), music
is made up of phenomena occurring on so many different levels of
reality and consciousness that capturing it all in a definition is
impossible. I suppose that it would be equally difficult for a
scientist to define science, a poet poetry or a painter painting –
though I'm not so sure about the last one. Your question is
indiscreet as well as difficult, because it invites me to give a quick
summary of the direction that my musical work, and thus my life,
has taken. I find that sort of thing rather embarrassing, and I
prefer to leave it to other people. I have tried doing it once or
twice, in interviews less important than this one, and I've always
regretted it afterwards, because I could never recognize myself in
what I had said: something was always missing. Anyway, I have
no vocation for oracular pronouncements. I have seen other
people trying to explain their music in terms of its "philosophy",
its "ideology", its "sociology" and its "politics", but all too often
they end up producing delirious verbal arabesques, which may
well tell us some interesting things about the author's personality
and neuroses, but not much about what he does, or has done, I
think that the easiest way for a musician to talk coherently about
himself is by talking about other people, about things that he has
around him, and behind him. A musical work always has an
impalpable zone with which we can only come to grips through
the mediating influence of works that we have already

assimilated. They don't necessarily have to be works that we identify with, but ones that we draw close to and observe – in other words, love – because they seem more richly impregnated with history than do other works, and because we find ourselves more freely able to invest them with what is perhaps the unrealized best of ourselves, and with a more open expression of our musical unconscious. Schumann writing about Chopin completed an imaginary self, Berlioz writing about Beethoven projected himself, Debussy writing about Mussorgsky described himself, as did Schoenberg writing on Brahms and Boulez on Berg. One can quite easily imagine Bach, seated at the harpsichord, discussing Couperin, or Mozart and Beethoven, seated at the fortepiano, discussing Bach. But to imagine Bach explaining his Violin Partitas, Mozart talking about his String Quintets, or Beethoven analyzing his *Fourth Symphony* for the benefit of court dignitaries is grotesque, indeed quite repulsive. Nobody would have thought of asking Beethoven what music was. But nowadays they do. So did I, for that matter, several years ago when – by way of introducing a series of television programmes – I asked ten or so musicians from Boulez to Cage, Milhaud, Stockhausen and Bernstein: *why music?*

D: It would be interesting to know why it is that, from Beethoven's death on, people began to talk and write about music so much.

B: Perhaps because music stopped being an objective activity designed to fulfil specific social functions and became, or at least was intended to be, the vehicle for expression and for personal ideas. Music deliberately embroiled itself in the universe of signs, as we would now call them, and of ideas. The composer became, like the poet and the painter, an "artist" whose ideals and whose world view appeared to disdain the artisan bric-a-brac of professional musicians. A distance was created between idea and musical practice which the more alert musicians felt obliged to try and explain to a new musical public: one that paid for their tickets and wanted to hear a symphony not once, but many times. This is where Aesthetics appeared, then as now coming to the rescue of those who talk and write about music. The composer began discussing his work and his aspirations at the point where in effect he stopped being a practical musician, a performer who had to work on his instrument almost every day. Chopin and Brahms, both great pianists, have left no writings. Nor indeed has that great organist Messiaen (his *Technique de mon langage musical* is embarrassing from the title on). But Schumann (who had injured a finger and couldn't play the piano any more), Berlioz (who played the guitar badly), Wagner and Schoenberg (who were by no means virtuosi on their respective instruments, piano and cello), have left behind a significant body of writings. It's a topic worthy of at least one doctoral thesis from a Sociology faculty (what it's really about, after all, is the distinction between intellectual labour and manual labour). And don't forget that, since Beethoven, all aspects of the creative process, even the most insignificant ones, have begun to acquire a price: the composer's manuscripts, the composer's glasses, the composer's postcard, the composer's bed, his school report, his house, his chair, his habits and, naturally, his interviews.

Trying to define music – which in any case is not an object, but a process – is rather like trying to define poetry: it's an operation made happily impossible by the futility of trying to establish the boundary between what is music and what isn't, or between poetry and non-poetry. Though there's the difference that with poetry the implicit distinction between language and literature, spoken language and written language, makes the boundary easier to define. Perhaps that's just what music is: the search for a boundary that is continually being shifted. In previous centuries, for instance, the tonal "boundary" marked out precise and profound territory. Nowadays the territories are enormous, and the boundaries as mobile and diverse as they have ever been. In fact, often the object of musical research and creation is not even the definition of a perceptual, expressive and conceptual boundary, but rather the moving of the boundaries as such. And in this case, paradoxically, it is much easier to answer your question: music is everything that one listens to with the intention of listening to music.

D: Do you think that this definition, drawn from the experience of a European musician, can be extended to other epochs and cultures?

B: In other cultures the boundaries are more stable. In many cases the problem of boundaries doesn't even arise because the problems of cultural relationships, relationships within musical production and music as art don't arise either: there are no territories to separate, and even the idea of music doesn't exist. For instance, among the Banda-Linda of Central Africa, whose music has been studied by the Israeli musicologist Simha Arom, there exist only concrete and specific activities (beating, blowing, singing and dancing) defined by religious and social functions. Their activities with sound are thus part of a social contract that is both obvious and – if the Banda-Linda and their ethnomusic-ologist friends will forgive me for saying so – rather elementary. What can't be related to a basic clapped rhythm, shared explicitly by everyone, has no sense for them. I find it interesting to try and grasp the functions of these collective, unanimous languages which maintain their existences independently of the individuals who activate them (normally until the radio, or some socio-economic trauma arrives to desecrate them) – just as if they were natural phenomena. Listening to these forms of behaviour, I sometimes have a vague sense of observing nature as it laboriously turns itself into culture, and the "raw" on the point of becoming "cooked". But leaving metaphors aside, one certainly gets the impression at times of catching a glimpse of certain *universals* of Western music – as in the pre-polyphonic techniques, the "hockets" of Central Africa, fixed within their boundaries. Whereas our composer, a creative artist who is eternally a "young man", intent upon giving form to "the uncreated conscience of his race", is like a navigator passing through the boundaries of his own history to explore unknown archipelagos, and to land on mysterious islands which he thinks he is the first to discover, and which he describes to others in sound. The richer his under-standing, the harder it is for him to steer his course.

When there is no unanimous social contract behind the making of and listening to music – such as there was during the baroque epoch, and indeed among the Banda-Linda of Bokassa – then you get almost as many ways of understanding music as there are people coming into contact with it. Each of these ways may be more or less simple, more or less knowledgeable, but in itself it will always be correct: you can describe it in a relatively precise manner, you can isolate its parameters and, if you have the patience, you can form them into a code. But even so, the teeming totality of these ways of listening won't give you a global and synthetic image of musical experience. It's rather like trying to put across the meaning of Life, God and Humanity. If I were a believer and you asked me what I understand by God, I'd reply that I don't know, that God must of necessity manifest himself within man, but that what men do and think is not God. The same is true of music's role in the world: it manifests itself in so many ways and has so many different functions, yet these ways and functions by themselves don't constitute music. It's a very important and salutary paradox, one that is a driving force behind the human world where feeling and knowledge are often incompatible. If it were possible to give a complete and definitive reply to your question it would mean that the very complex, but also somewhat mysterious process which music is had come to an end, leaving us with nothing better to do than join the tricksters who celebrate the death of music and the reign of silence. And this death would signal many other deaths, because it would be like replying definitively to the ever-open question of how man relates to the world through his signs and symbols. It would mean renouncing a creative vision of that relationship, which is always there, waiting to be established – *toujours recommencée*, like Valéry's sea. Just imagine a world – ours, not the Pigmies' – in which questions of how social forces interact with music's many dimensions don't arise because we've already got an answer for everything, rather like a market survey, and there's nothing more to discover except a few new computer sounds. Or imagine a world suddenly filled with Eisler's music – if he'd written enough, that is – because he knew everything, he had an answer for everything and was quite capable of telling you in a few brusque words what music is and what it's for.

Perhaps you could say the same about music as about every other human experience – though there aren't that many of them, in fact – that by harmonizing and transforming nature and culture it is both practical and empirical, but at the same time it involves us on the deepest levels. That is to say that in music the empirical, sense-oriented dimension on one side and the intellectual and spiritual dimension on the other – body and soul as our ancestors would have said – become identified in a system of relations which we are forever patiently putting to the test, even though at times they seem obscure to our inner ears. Excuse my rhetoric, but perhaps one can only get round a lethal question like yours with a witty paradox in the manner of Umberto Eco or a calm, careful analysis in the style of a humanistic scholar like Massimo Mila: but then, they can permit themselves to take a step outside music and look at it as if it were a hen who's laid an egg . . .

D: What do you think is the best way of coming to grips with such a vast and complex experience?

B: I think that all ways of making, listening to and even talking about music are right in their way. When music has sufficient complexity and semantic depth, it can be approached and understood in different ways. Most commercial songs, and for that matter the sonic wallpaper and the musical tombolas of the self-styled avant-garde, can only be listened to on one level: but there's also music that can be heard on many levels, and is continually generating musical meaning. The more simple and one-dimensional a musical discourse is, the more diffuse and immediate its relationship to everyday reality. The more concentrated and complex it is, the more complex and selective are its social relations, and the more ramified its meanings. So that a song can express a moment of human work and emotion, and it is an immediately "useful" instrument to people at different times of the day or year: but you can replace one with another. Whereas complex musical works are irreplaceable moments in a historical process. Think of Beethoven and Schoenberg: their musical thought often seems to have a positively excessive semantic depth. There's enough for everyone, and always a bit left over which remains in the shadows, waiting for a different approach. I don't believe people when they say "I don't understand this music, will you explain it to me?". It means they don't understand themselves and the place they occupy in the world, and that it doesn't occur to them that music is also a product of collective life. Sometimes I have a strange feeling that musical processes can be more intelligent than the people who produce and listen to them; that the cells of those processes, like the chromosomes of a genetic code, can be more intelligent than the perceptive organs that should be making sense of them. It's as if music were miming one of the most incredible of natural processes: the passage from inanimate to animate life, from molecular to organic forms, from an abstract and immobile dimension to a vital and expressive one. Music must be capable of educating people to discover and create relations between different elements (as Dante said in the *Convivio*, "music is all relative"), and in doing that it speaks of the history of man and of his musical resources in all their acoustic, and expressive aspects. I'm interested by music that creates and develops relations between very distant points, and pursues a very wide transformational trajectory (Beethoven's *Diabelli Variations*, for instance). The listener has to be aware that there are different ways of grasping the sense of that trajectory, just as there are different ways of experiencing an encounter, however transitory, between the practical level of life and the deepest levels within the individual. I must emphasize that music cannot detach itself from gestures, techniques, ways of saying and doing – but it's not exhausted by them, and because it is both thought and practice, it realizes a unity that does indeed transcend the opposition between the senses and the understanding. That is why music is a precious instrument but often a difficult one, particularly for those who *only* listen to it.

D: When one asks a composer these sorts of question one expects a reply that is in some way oriented towards production. But you've devoted much of your time to talking about the effects that music has on people. One might say that although you are a "producer", you have chosen to define music from the point of view of the "receiver".

B: I probably have. But I don't think that "producer" and "receiver" can be easily separated. There's less historical distance between a musical work and the person listening to it than there is between a picture and the person looking at it. Musical works aren't covered by that "great master's varnish", in other words, the varnish of time, which places great paintings at a certain distance from us. Great musical works of the past are being continually "remade" and reinterpreted, even if we have to transcribe them and make them sound on completely different instruments. It's part of their nature that this should happen. But one mustn't forget that the industrial demands placed upon music have fetichized and formalized its means. Once, orchestras were rather "open" groups of musicians. A Haydn symphony could be performed in the same year with fifty violins in London and with twelve in Dresden. In other words, music needs interpreters, and this fact alone makes the relation between "production" and "reception" almost inextricable. Such eminent ladies as Gisèle Brelet and Susanne Langer have occupied themselves with the problem, but frankly it doesn't much interest me. All I can say is that I don't greatly like those two terms ("production" and "reception") because they suggest a factory churning out musical consumer products for people to buy and eat. Maybe my aversion for them is over-instinctive and visceral – and anyway, I like to think that a fisherman or a farm-labourer are producers of culture at least as much as are a bureaucrat or a television announcer. The musician and the listener don't belong to two different socio-cultural categories. I am a composer, but I'm also a listener – indeed, as far as I'm concerned, I'm the best audience I know. I'm the incarnation of an ideal audience.

D: This vision of an audience whose "incarnation" you feel yourself to be must mean that a certain section of the general category of listeners certainly can't be identified with, or indeed even be assimilated into the Berio audience.

B: I don't know, maybe. But it's obvious that the term audience is rather general: it's rather like talking about tourists, wives, patients, Aryans . . . What I want to emphasize is that the creative musical process implies listening, whether solitary or public, and that even talking and writing about music, as we are now doing, always implies a history of possible ways of listening. But might I add that my ideal public is one with many faces, all bringing different motivations to their encounter with the music. A public that is the very opposite of the one, say, that you used to find at Bayreuth, and that might take over again now that the Chereau-Boulez Ring Cycle has come and gone, or among the subscribers at any large opera house. Dividing the public up into categories isn't necessarily so relevant to music as it is to the music industry, which certainly does distinguish people according to their real or virtual buying power. If we leave the problems of musical education on one side – since they deserve separate discussion, and even when you allow for their negative aspects, they don't have the sort of immediate influence on the general listening public that industrial operations do – then, as I said before, in my view everyone understands music in their own fashion. I don't even think that there's a right and a wrong way of listening to it: just more simple and more complex ones. For example, one way of reading Wagner is based entirely on harmonic or erotic considerations, whereas in another transcendental one, which scans the music in broad sweeps, eroticism becomes the ritual of a universal renunciation of life. Some ways of listening are induced by the music industry, others are the result of long interior maturation. There are revelations (young people suddenly discovering Vivaldi, Mahler and certain areas of contemporary music), and individual, élitist conquests based on long familiarity and a concern to clarify relations between historically diverse aesthetic values. There are those who approach music through the performance and interpretation market (the Beethoven of Michelangeli, Pollini, Brendel or Barenboim etc.). There are the old musicologists – either acidulated or comatose – and the young champions of linguistics who sacrifice the best years of their lives in order to squeeze a generative grammar out of a Mozart minuet. And so on: both the anecdotal and the real aspects of listening are infinite. But within that infinite variety (which embraces composer, performer and listener) I don't think you can make *a priori* distinctions. Certainly, an intelligent writer can suggest a particular focus of attention, which will open up further levels of listening within the work in a sort of cognitive spiral . . . But if someone listening to a Beethoven symphony picks out from the complex strategy of relationships only the most obvious elements like the melodies (when there are any), that doesn't strike me as a profanation (and anyway, I'm afraid there are plenty of famous performers who do the same thing). One can only regret that many people have not have been able to exercise their brains and ears in order to intuit or to understand what a melody in Bach or Beethoven implies. The fact is that, like almost all music, the work of Beethoven or Bach allows for that way of listening among others. It's rather like only paying attention to the rhetorical aspects without which discussion becomes ineffective. One day a friend of mine went to a talk given by Sanguineti. It was marvellous, she told me. Sanguineti spoke superbly. You could have heard a pin drop. It was absolutely fascinating – and amusing too. I asked what he had been talking about. "Ah, I don't know," she replied. In other words, she had been listening to the melodies, not to their deeper function.

D: So could one say that your first definition of music as something that establishes harmony between practical behaviour and intellectual processes can accommodate any approach to music that allows this effect to be achieved?

B: I would think so. But the important thing, as far as I'm concerned, is not to apply moral judgements to people who listen to music in one way or another. It's only when you adopt political criteria and try to view musical experiences as an expression of class relations that you can't avoid moral judgements: and they will of necessity come down heavily on a society that encourages people to listen to melodies and nothing else. That's one reason why, at a certain point in our history, melodies broke up into little pieces.

D: Do you agree with Adorno's analysis of the "categories" into which listeners can be divided?

B: No, although it's not easy to completely refute anything that Adorno writes – he was, after all, one of the most acute, and also most negative intellects to excavate the creativity of the past 150 years. I rather suspect that the "classes" and "categories" that Adorno described in such a detailed and specific fashion no longer exist, and indeed never did exist – not at any rate in the paroxismically alienated form that he analyzed. Just as the sociologically specific meaning for individual works that he moralistically implied has never existed either. But at the same time, the description that Adorno gives of the various different types of listeners is rather too close to a rigid sociological analysis of the way choices are made, not about a specific object, like a utilitarian Fiat, a truck or a Maserati, but about the combustion engine. In other words, Adorno seems incensed about the choice of the combustion engine in general, rather than about the choice of a car that can or cannot get him to Cologne in two hours. So he takes offence at all commercial and consumer music and not, say, Gershwin or the Beatles. In other words, he attacks categories so general that they seem removed from any dynamic of transformation. He forgets that one of the most cunning and interesting aspects of consumer music, the mass media, and indeed of capitalism itself, is their fluidity, their unending capacity for adaptation and assimilation. Adorno's vision is of a society united in evil, where all forms of behaviour, art, consumer spending, politics – are socially and historically predetermined, and mirror each other with relentless negativity right up into the most rarefied regions of his thought. And then, at the heart of it all, there's always that monolithic, teutonic, and basically rather fetichistic conception of the musical work that diminishes the credibility of his picturesque study of listening habits. The musical work as Adorno sees it becomes the meeting-place for universal impossibilities, frustrations and contradictions.

If you look back - or rather down from the inaccessible heights of Adorno's thought - you become dizzy: in fact I think you'd be rather hard put to it to establish a clear and necessary relationship between the tragic, picturesque and anecdotal socio-musical vision that springs so generously from his ardent imagination and the global conception of musical experience towards which, as a good Hegelian, he was aiming. To say, for instance, that the music of Schoenberg or Webern terrifies not because it is incomprehensible, but only because it gives form to anguish and fright (from which right-thinking people only manage to save themselves through regression) seems to me an over-optimistic and reductionist statement. Who knows, maybe Adorno, with his tendency not to "represent" musical reality as it appears from moment to moment, but instead to continuously transcend it, expresses one of the most fascinating and complex aspects of Jewish culture, which does indeed lean towards transcendence and avoids reducing "experiences" (including that of God) to pronounceable words and symbols - though it may still interpret them. In Adorno the two levels - "empirical" observation of musical facts and theoretical, holistic induction - tend not to communicate, or communicate primarily through dramatic and synthetic gestures. But once he has taken off into theoretical realms, he seems to me ill-advised to put his feet back on the ground and deduce "empirical" confirmations from the *opera omnia* of Schoenberg and Webern while limiting himself, strangely enough, to *Pulcinella* when dealing with Stravinsky. When Adorno writes that the only authentic musical works are those that measure up to the most extreme forms of horror, he is lying, and he ends up aristocratically exploiting horror. Apparently it is a specific, even a day-by-day measure of horror, but effectively this is horror as seen by the New School for Social Research, - a place rich in sociological delights, no doubt, but also, symptomatically, a worthy haven for Eisler's musical "stupidity". Adorno permits himself a snobbish vision of horror, a horror that strangely disregards the idea of need. I can't say that I've read all of Adorno, but it seems to me that within his universe there's no room for an awareness of need – the whole range of human needs in the widest, most tragic and least consumer-oriented sense of the word. As a philosopher of music Adorno is a great aphorist. He manages to apply the filter of Schoenbergian poetics to music of all times and types. In a strange, contradictory fashion, Adorno's apocalyptic musical vision tends to lose all contact with every-day reality, as if the sole and ultimate destiny of every piece of music was to contribute to an epistemology of music.

My hackles rise when I hear young Italian would-be-Adornos passing summary and disdainful judgement on those large portions of humanity who dare to acknowledge a consolatory dimension in music. Music can symbolically represent possible orders and disorders, different paths that can be pursued through real life – the concrete life of ideas and sentiments. So why should music not also console someone? Personally I'm not at all interested in using music for consolation, just as I'm not interested in using Cézanne's paintings for decorative purposes, but I don't see why someone who, sadly, has no other option should not engage with music through that rather indistinct and flaccid sentiment, consolation. You never know, that road might one day lead him to Beethoven's Op.132 *Dankgesang*. Just think of the wave of interest in music that there's been over the past ten years or so among young people, who find themselves in a rather complex and dramatic world whose workings they have often lacked the means (ideological means included) to decipher. I'm sure that many people are attracted to music because they sense, however dimly, that it can indeed symbolize the possibility of a consolatory and, who knows, even a utopian interpretation of the world. In music the onward flow of history, of which more sensitive people are continually aware, is transcribed into different times and dimensions. Music allows young people to move into an alternative space – not necessarily a reassuring and optimistic one, because it is partially determined by the real world, both inner and outer. However, anyone entering that space can in some measure adapt it to his own needs, and even creatively live there – taking it as an image of the world and consoling himself with it . . . It's very encouraging to see concert-halls these days full of young people who'll listen to anything and everything. But as yet it seems to me a difficult phenomenon to analyze, even on a consolatory level. And a marxist analysis would be impossible.

D: What do you mean by a marxist analysis?

B: I should really be talking about a "marxist sociology", by which I mean the observation of mass phenomena primarily as processes of reification amongst which move, larva-like, market-oriented individuals. Neither the large number of people getting involved with music these days, nor the smaller number who keep away from it can be identified in terms of class, or defined on the basis of economic relations. I think that we're dealing more with cultural relations in the widest and most inclusive sense – and that takes in economic and class relations. Clearly the mass media and a different way of organizing musical life have made music more accessible. But it's too easy just to attribute the current phenomenon of a great, indiscriminate move towards music to industry's desire for a wider market, or a more responsible organizing and programming of musical activities. Whether you observe the publics of "trivial" music, concerts and opera separately, or take them *in toto* as an indiscriminate mass of music consumers, I think that the phenomenon escapes precise analysis – including the marxist type which, in musical matters, tends to be dogmatic and simplistic. It tends, that is, to create the illusion that music written today can reveal an idea of the social world with the same criteria and the same conclusiveness as music written 150 years ago, which has had plenty of time to clarify and decant its relations with the world. Indeed, a self-styled marxist critique is often a mass of contradictions: if it takes its eyes off the past, which is its province, and scrutinizes the present, then music

positively *disappears* and the accounts don't balance any more . . .
This non-coincidence between ideology and behaviour, historical conditioning and class conditioning, abstract and concrete
work, intellectual and manual work is certainly nothing new in
music (that's precisely why, as I was saying earlier, so much has
been written about music since the last century), and it's even less
so in the general field of human work; in political, or rather party-
political work, the distance has taken on dramatic proportions.
Adorno was the first to discern and analyze this mismatch, this
alienation in music's social substance. But when he had to give a
real musical example, Adorno's moralistic impulses led him
towards an unwise target: Igor Stravinsky. For my own part, I
hope that my work is one possible reply to the various fractures
that exist within musical work; fractures that fascinate rather
than worry me, because they oblige me to explore terrain that is
creatively uninhabited as far as music is concerned, to move
beyond antinomies of a moralistic type where there are good guys
on one side and bad guys on the other.

*D: Is music still to be lamented as the Cinderella of the arts, or do you think
that nowadays it has a role in the cognitive growth of the non-specialist, the
man in the street?*

B: Yes, maybe. Anyway, it's obvious that the edifice of our culture
would make no sense without the bricks and pillars of music. But
the role of the ideas expressed in music is more virtual than real.
Nothing will ever happen in music to parallel what happened
around Mondrian's work, when he started by creating purified
geometric forms from trees, and finished up profoundly
influencing architectural thought. Without Mondrian, Park
Avenue wouldn't be the same. But I don't think music has ever
been the Cinderella of the arts. Indeed, nowadays music
obviously permeates the life of your "non-specialist", even if
he's not aware of it.

But I don't believe that such a cognitive growth can be
explained and codified in books: I assume anyway that they will
never be written, and even if they were, they would be illegible

and tautological because they would have to presuppose too much of what they sought to demonstrate. But returning to our "non-specialist" who can, or should have, music as part of his cognitive growth, I think that listening to music tends to fill an empty space that is continually reforming in him: not a negative or passive emptiness, but an active one – a sort of feminine space of the spirit that is there to be filled, precisely, by our cognitive growth. I sometimes feel that listening to a performance is like being penetrated and invaded by music, and I have the sensation of an emptiness finally filled.

D: Have you noticed how our "non-specialist", who is well educated, buys records and even goes to concerts, when he has to speak about music, often feels obliged to add "though really I don't know a thing about it"?

B: Perhaps that's because most people, especially in Italy, have never broken the ice by learning to play an instrument, studying a little music and learning to sing well. But there's also an objective difficulty in verbalizing musical experience, so that the non-specialist in particular must have continual recourse to metaphor.

D: But if the same person had to talk about painting, he wouldn't feel at all uncomfortable, and could quite easily bluff his way through.

B: Perhaps he'd have learnt that from the painters themselves who, with one or two notable exceptions, tend to free-wheel when they start talking. But clearly the experience of painting, even abstract painting, is always linked to a concrete reality which exists independently of the intentions of the observer. Both the concepts and the physical materials of painting have a sense even if you detach them from the meanings that they convey because they exist outside pictorial experience: colours, canvas, sands, lacquers, wood, plastic and spatial delimitation are all things that exist in everyday life and offer themselves to the painter without apparent mediation. Whereas you won't find the sounds of musical instruments in nature nor in everyday life: you have to learn to produce them with elaborate and rather difficult techniques. I suppose it's because of this that there's a semiology of the visual arts but no real semiology of music. There is a certain symmetry in the relationship between sight and hearing on the one hand, and looking and listening on the other: apart from anything else, because the second couple implies a will to perceive with eyes and ears. But there's a great difference between each couple: it's perfectly normal to close your eyes when you don't want to see, but it's rather strange, even dramatic, to block your ears to avoid hearing. The ear is the organ of space and time, and it's always listening to and locating something. You can't "distract the ear", it forces on you a continuous distribution and placing of what is audible: it is psychologically more complex and "open" than looking. It is also more difficult to talk about. Perhaps the painters should read that marvellous study, *Listening* (*Ascolto*) that Roland Barthes wrote for the *Enciclopedia Einaudi*. And to balance things out, musicians ought to read Paul Klee's *Das bildnerische Denken*.

But, certainly, music always puts up a considerable resistance to being "translated" into words, even though talking about music can be part of the creative process. We live in a world of written words, and what cannot be written down is often distorted or simply ceases to exist. It's by no means uncommon for musicians to blithely refer to a non-European music as "improvised" simply because it isn't written down. More and more often I read texts on music that have nothing to do with a real musical experience, nor even with a musical project: they are verbal paraphrases of musical realities. The idiotic prose to which the presenters of exhibitions have accustomed us often infiltrates writings on music. Who knows, maybe it's because of a fear of meaning and an inability to reconcile reality with their own vision of the world, maybe it's a fear that music is also alienated labour, completely cut off from or imprisoned by relations of production, and that it therefore needs to be protected by a smoke screen of words, by a verbal illusion of order. Maybe it's because music is not as immediately effective a political instrument as painting and poetry, maybe it's a need to express and represent *ipso facto* which is more important than listening to the sounds of a voice, maybe it's authentic existential anguish, maybe, maybe ... But for instance, it's a fact that there's no use in trying to find relationships between the totally private verbal delirium of certain musicians and their scores, which are often full of good sense. Perhaps it's the fault of Adorno once again: that great advocate in the High Court of music, frustrated artist, and shaper of poetics. It is he who has so tirelessly managed to invent, through words, a set of convincing relationships between the universal and the particular. In fact, his writings on music are also a metamusic, a work of art, where ideas proliferate from ideas and not necessarily from musical reality.

D: Whose writings on music interest you most?

B: Those of Boulez – another great advocate. His writings are exemplary and useful not only for their intrinsic value, but also for the reactions that they arouse in the historicist camp when he starts weighing up the pros and cons of history. Boulez has a mania for weighing things up and, like Adorno, he tends to let ideas proliferate from ideas: but the centre of his concerns remains obdurately musical – even if it's often a music that doesn't exist. His world has an extraordinary coherence and transparency whether he writes, conducts the music of this century or pulls the strings of musical power. It is remarkable that, even in his writings, he has succeeded in putting ascetic parentheses around history, and in pursuing "*l'être absolument moderne*", though without the dry blood of a season in hell on his face ...

In Italy it's Massimo Mila who has always interested me. Perhaps this is because he is not merely a critic and a musicologist as far as I'm concerned. He has accompanied me throughout my musical development, even though I was not always aware of it. He resists musical fashions, loves music deeply, and expresses that love without snobbery but with the backing of vast cultural resources that save him from visceral reactions to the music and the musicians of his time. And then I'm grateful to him for his fidelity to the memory of Bruno Maderna.

D: Radio, television, advertising, records etc. create a continuous wall of sound around us which inevitably affect the formation of our tastes, even if we're not really aware of them as cultural experiences. It's a commonplace that the average person's musical choices are largely induced by the culture industry's use of the mass media, and that consumption can be differentiated according to age and social class. What relationship do you have with these channels and their programming?

B: That's a lot to ask – perhaps you'd get a better answer from Umberto Eco who has studied the problems of mass communication in depth. But you're presumably referring to programming on Italian radio and television networks which I must confess I don't know much about since I hardly watch Italian television at all.

But I did a lot of work for television between 1971 and 1973 when, along with Vittoria Ottolenghi and Gianfranco Mingozzi, I prepared a series of twelve broadcasts on music called "*C'è musica e musica*" ("There's music and music"). It was fascinating work, and the results seem to have worked well because it's been rebroadcast in many different places round the world. Our objective was to introduce the average viewer to what goes on inside the heads of those who make, study and love music. Each programme was treated as a musical form (I did most of the editing myself on the moviola, and I remember that Stockhausen wanted me to make a score of it), and thus managed to focus the viewer's attention on the rather diversified, and often complex arguments dealt with by such musicians as Bernstein, Dallapiccola, Ligeti, Mila, Copland, Nono, Messiaien, Maderna, Berberian, Cage, Boulez, etc. A lot of music was heard in "*C'è musica e musica*", and I'm sure that at the time it helped to develop the viewers' musical tastes. I think that is the main function of the mass media when they are used courageously and responsibly: helping people's taste and capacity for choice to evolve – as well as simply supplying information without cultural intimidation.

But I must admit that the theoretical problems surrounding music on radio, television and records aren't very central to my interests even though, as you rightly say, they have a great influence on the musical choices that people make – and even though I'm often involved with all of them myself. Overall it's a very complex problem. There are privileged people (like you and me) whose education or social position allows them to avoid the direct influence of the mass media, but there are also people unable to make their own choices, and protect themselves from the inevitably negative aspects of mass culture. It's no use getting indignant about the mass media: they're a part of reality like aeroplanes and telephones. It's much better to try and help create conditions in which the mass media are not excessively fetichized, but are instead accepted and used for what in effect they are, in other words, as instruments of information (and therefore education) and of entertainment, rather than of cultural brutalization and political power.

D: But isn't the situation within the record market a more complicated one? Listening to the radio may indeed be a matter of a moment's relaxation, but buying a record, especially for young people, means spending quite a bit of money, and because it involves a precise choice, it indicates a precise cultural orientation.

B: I suppose that's true. But I have no precise opinions in the matter, and it's not a problem that I think about much because, no matter how you look at it, you can never get to the heart of it. Being "cleaner" than radio or television, maybe the record is a meeting-point between élite musical culture, mass musical culture and the music industry. The interaction between these three is terribly complicated and riddled with contradictions, and it partially mirrors a society where cultural demands are less conditioned by what's on offer than we are sometimes led to believe.

D: Do you think that the record industry has an effect upon the musical formation of young people?

B: I can only repeat what everyone knows, in other words, that records are an invaluable aid to musical education and can certainly help to speed up studies in composition and musicology. I say that although, in fact, I listen to records very rarely. But no-one should underestimate the pedagogical value of records, provided they are not used to make matters simpler and conceptually poorer. Forgive me if I begin, as I often do, by looking back . . . Consider for example that, before Berlioz, there were no real treatises on instrumentation. Musicians from Monteverdi to Brahms learnt pragmatically, from experience. They adapted themselves to the often unforeseen situations by which they found themselves confronted, and resolved them via common sense (as well as their own genius, naturally). It's not by chance that the first real treatise on instrumentation, the first inventory of instrumental experiences, was written by Berlioz at a moment when the orchestra's timbre resources were beginning to explode, as did instrumental techniques, harmonic strategies, intensity of sound, the quantity of listeners, the quality of the spaces in which music was performed and the activities of the music market. Even common sense was about to explode into a multitude of individual senses. It was inevitable that someone should try to coordinate and stabilize the instrumental practice of the time with the help of a treatise (thus allowing for a greater exchange of ideas). Our own century has seen explosions of an altogether different order, and a traditionally conceived treatise, which does not address itself to all aspects of composition and their reciprocal influences with equal responsibility, would turn into a book of recipes for sound-tracks with a few strange fingerings for wind instruments and a few other anecdotal devices. If you wanted a really useful treatise nowadays, you would have to transform it into something nearer to an encyclopedia with chapters on instrumental acoustics, timbre and harmony, timbre and instrumental register, timbre and speed of articulation, acoustic and psycho-acoustic instrumental kinship, voice and instruments, amplified instruments, electro-acoustic transform-ations of instruments, etc. You'd also have to discuss each instrument within a contemporary perspective – one, that is, which takes clear account of the fact that orchestral timbres, no longer being fused together by natural harmonic resonance, have "liberated" themselves. In fact, what I'm talking about is a project – we nicknamed it "the bible" – that I had sketched out with Boulez a few years ago for IRCAM and Universal Edition, though it never got beyond the stage of good intentions. Anyway, in this extremely rich, articulated, chaotic and acoustically unpredictable situation, records can partially, though only partially, take the place of our ancestors' practice and common sense – a good sense based above all on experience and a good ear, and on being able to quickly absorb what was going on around them. Naturally I'm talking about practical, rather than conceptual and theoretical good sense. And I'm not speaking from experience because I'd been through my musical training before I came in contact with records. I was eighteen when I heard my first record at a friend's house. It was in 1943, and we had to listen to it secretly because it was traditional jazz from New Orleans, which was banned by the fascist regime. It was like listening to the BBC.

D: Nowadays we seem to be witnessing a revival of interest in old music. How do you explain the numbers of young people that we see at evenings of renaissance or baroque music, or subscribing to a whole cycle of concerts dedicated to the organ music of Bach, for example? What does this ready response mean? I would have thought that many of these events were fairly demanding even for a professional musician, and they are far removed from the cultural expressions of contemporary society. What do you make of this "return to the past"?

B: This is a question that could only be asked by an Italian. You have only to go to England, Germany or America to see that Bach has been close to young people there for many years. Anyhow, as an Italian I can assure you that this is not a "return to the past" because many of those young people are unaware of Bach's existence, and even more have no historical awareness, or taste, for musical chronology. For many young Italian people twenty years ago, the "cool" improvisations "à la Bach" of the blind pianist Tristano and real Bach were practically the same thing.

And the same goes for real Mozart and Mozart sung as an eight-voice "ba-da-ba-da-ba-da" by the Swingle Singers. I think that this business of discovering Bach is linked rather more closely to the rediscovery by young people of the practical dimension of music-making. This is made possible by using relatively simple baroque music that can survive "translation" onto instruments such as the recorder, which can be played with a minimum of technique: music where the rhythmic discourse confirms and reinforces the harmonic discourse, which does the same for the melodic discourse, and so on – creating such coherence that any one of those discourses can evoke the others, which are more or less implicit in it. Another aspect of Bach that makes him attractive to young people in Italy is that it is almost always easy to understand which are the structurally significant notes and which are the decorative ones (so that those works by Bach where the two dimensions interpenetrate – such as the *Goldberg Variations* that Beethoven loved so much – are rather remote from the interests of young people). It is this clear division of roles among the notes that has, among other things, stimulated rudimentary attempts at improvisation in a baroque style, and the formation of little "baroque" groups that are helping, even in Italy, to recover that enormously important dimension of home music-making which seemed lost, but which is absolutely fundamental. Anyone who really loves music needs a practical relation with it, as we can see from children, who are always very pragmatic, and begin to do things before they understand them . . . Making music together like this is a very positive thing, and reminds me of what it meant for me to listen to my father when he was making music at home with his friends – and then to play with him and other musicians the whole extraordinary repertoire of chamber music, from Mozart to Brahms. I think that this rediscovery of the pleasure of music-making is very interesting indeed, even though it sometimes takes on some odd forms, such as improvising with those horrible gadgets, synthesizers.

D: Why do you define synthesizers as "horrible gadgets", given that you are so receptive to the resources that modern technology offers on the instrumental level?

B: Because they're not musical instruments – something quite different. Maybe I exaggerate when I call them gadgets because they are very clever systems based on the voltage control of oscillators, which have simplified the switch from the old analogue techniques to the current, and highly evolved digital technologies. The fact is that commercial synthesizers aspire to be musical maids-of-all-work, and because of their specific characteristics they end up taking over from the composers who use them. A composer can't think musically with those machines, and ends up impoverished by them in one way or another. At best, they produce fascinating sound effects that help to accentuate one of the greatest problems of our time: the distance and the indifference between music's acoustic and conceptual dimensions. The best use that I've yet heard of synthesizers has been in America with Morton Subotnick, and with rock, disco and punk groups. Stockhausen tried to use one for *Sirius*, but it nearly drove him crazy, and he ended up using it as a generator of sound structures which he then elaborated, edited and superimposed on tape in the traditional fashion. One of the most alarming things about synthesizers is that they are not precise. One of the most interesting is that they are constructed on modular criteria, and are thus open, for better and for worse. But they're not musical instruments.

INTERVIEW 2

with Rossana Dalmonte

D: Just now you mentioned how important playing chamber music at home with your father had been in your development. How much did the family tradition influence your decision to take up music professionally?

B: I never really had to decide because I never had any doubts about it. My family background and the environment I lived in decided for me, in a way. I never had the problem of choosing whether to study law, architecture or medicine, as do so many young people after leaving high school. I veered slightly off course only once, at the age of 11, when my great love of the sea seemed to be leading me towards a nautical career. That was when I painted my self-portrait with the paints that were used for the garden railings – you can see it over there, with me standing next to a chair on which is placed, right in the foreground, a sailor's beret. This was my only moment of crisis. My earliest musical education took place at home and I am grateful to my father for this.

D: Superimposed on this background of family music there must have been other, more personal experiences: books that you read, things that you did for yourself.

B: Certainly there were, at school particularly. But music was the most important and formative feature of the family environment in which I lived until I was seventeen to eighteen years old. Up to a certain stage in my development I identified music with the personalities of my father Ernesto on the one hand, and of my grandfather Adolfo on the other. As a boy, I had an enormous admiration for my grandfather who was a rather unapproachable and egoistic man. He died at the age of 94 and had been completely blind for the last twenty years of his life. He was born in 1847, and I don't suppose it ever occurred to him that he was a contemporary of Brahms, or that he could have been Mahler's and Debussy's uncle and Schoenberg's father. He was an organist and composer, and he would boast that he had won all the organ improvisation competitions in Liguria. He loved Verdi and loathed Wagner. He wrote polkas, masses and waltzes dedicated to different royal families, and to the princesses of the various European courts as if he were quite one of the family, though in fact he'd hardly ever left Oneglia in his life. My grandfather wrote music which was excellent in its own way. His waltz duets, which my cousin and I would play for him on his birthday, are now first-rate kitsch. He was a very practical musician – unimpressed by fancy ideas. In family matters he was often heartless: my mother, Ada Dal Fiume Berio, bore the brunt of it.

My father was quite different. He also started his musical career very young. Even when he was a little boy, he was already playing the piano in light orchestras. I can still vaguely remember how he used to play the piano for silent films in a cinema in Oneglia. But his musical education was more thorough, more conventional and more middle class than my grandfather's. In other words, an education dictated primarily by conventions rather than by any real need. He attended the Milan Conservatory (where he found himself in the same class as De Sabata), and he also went to Parma to study with Pizzetti; he nurtured musical and intellectual ambitions very different from those of my grandfather. As well as a symphonic poem (which he dedicated, may God forgive him, to "the descendant of Augustus"), pieces for organ and a mass, he wrote an enormous number of pieces for voice and piano. Some of them are very attractive on an expressive level. But because of his ambitions, and of the setting in which they had taken shape, my father lacked that touch of authenticity which, at a much more basic musical level, had characterized my grandfather. My grandfather was a bit like homemade bread: rough and simple. Whereas my father was like bread from the baker's: more refined but less tasty. But it was bread, all the same. Happily, I realized pretty quickly that man does not live by bread alone. Anyhow, it's certainly true that I have always found it rather difficult to relate to my father's music: perhaps because I heard quite a lot of it coming into existence (my father composed at the piano). Or perhaps because private motivations and colorations in music generally leave me cold, not only in other people's work, but also in my own. It seems to me that only humour and sarcasm can redeem the explicit presence of "private" elements in music. Clearly I don't find it easy to put my family reminiscences in order, or to reconcile myself to musical life in the provinces during those years.

D: But perhaps it wasn't just provincial life. Don't forget what all musical life was like in Italy during those two decades.

B: True enough, but at the time I was in no position to realize that, and I lived off whatever I could lay my hands on. The radio, which broadcast mainly opera, was my only link with the outside world. We listened to it a lot, perhaps too much. In fact, it was a lunch-time broadcast of *La Bohème* that was responsible for a very embarrassing moment. I was about thirteen at the time, and I suddenly found my eyes filling with tears. So, to hide them, I dropped a spoon on the floor. . . Anyway, I got over the emotional excitements of *La Bohème*. As well as the radio, there was my father who ensured that the house was full of opera through his numerous singing students. There weren't any public concerts in Oneglia, only a few badly performed operas. Before I was fifteen I had only heard one symphony concert, but that was at the Casino in San Remo. It was conducted by Gino Marinuzzi, and the programme included a *Rhapsody* by Gino Marinuzzi junior for saxophone and orchestra, with an "obbligato" piano part. Gino himself played the piano part, and I was full of admiration and sincere envy. I must have conducted the first concert in the history of Oneglia myself in 1976, with the London Sinfonietta. But apart from a few special events like the shows put on by Grock, the clown (Adriano Wettach), and apart from the few enlightened people to be found there, the cultural horizons of Oneglia were, and still are, limited to two things: oil and pasta.

During those years at home in Oneglia there was, however, one oasis of absolute musical happiness: the chamber music that my father often performed at home, with excellent players almost all of whom traded in oil, soap and the like. One of them, Pippo Giovannetti, with whom I studied the violin for three years, had even in his youth been a pupil of Vaša Prihoda. All this music at home gave me the chance to become very familiar with the whole range of chamber music, with and without piano: Mozart, Beethoven, Schubert, Schumann, Mendelssohn, Brahms and even Dvořák. The relatively mild climate of the Ligurian hills (Grock had built himself an improbable tropical-oriental villa slightly higher up, and Christian Democratic cement had not yet invaded the area) made it possible, even in winter, to carry on playing with the window open onto the garden until two or three in the morning. When I was still a child I would fall asleep, earlier of course, on a pile of cushions which I had prudently arranged under a table. Later on, I started to play myself. I remember my emotive baptism with the *Trio in C minor* from Beethoven's op. 1 and the 'Rondo alla Zingarese' from Brahms's *Piano Quartet in G minor.*

D: So it's true to say that your training was, from the very beginning, rigorously classical, and that it continued in the same vein when you entered the Milan Conservatory. I believe that Ghedini was one of your teachers?

B: Yes, but that was later on – and my years with Ghedini were to be all-important. But my first real teacher at the Conservatory was Giulio Cesare Paribeni, Professor of Counterpoint and Fugue, and an excellent man, kind, sensitive and strict. Before getting a place at the Conservatory, I went to visit him at his house and brought him, among other things, a *Preludio a una festa marina* for strings, and he told me that it seemed to him like a "cinema" because it jumped from one idea to another without any sense of necessity. I passed a week of terror convinced that he wouldn't let me sit the fourth-year harmony exams.

D: You have spoken about your musical training with its two dimensions, opera and chamber music. But there clearly must have been a time when you began reading about things that were not specifically musical.

B: Of course, through a conventional education at junior school and high school. But at the same time I threw myself into exploring other things off the beaten track such as *Hedda Gabler*, and *The Master Builder* (I even tried my hand at writing an Ibsen-style drama). And then I read Rainer Maria Rilke (in 1945 I composed a cantata for soprano and orchestra based on his *Annunciation*). I read and re-read *The Notebooks of Malte Laurids Brigge*, which perhaps I still carry around with me somewhere in the back of my mind. So much so that, now that I am working with Calvino on a new music theatre project on the theme of listening (suggested by Barthes), the 'Notebooks' keep resurfacing – particularly those obsessive episodes of deciphering and inter-preting the "sounds from the room next door". I had got to know Bergson, above all through the writings of Lorenzo Giusso who was Professor of Philosophy at the University of Naples. In fact, towards the end of 1945 I set off on a long and adventurous journey to Naples to meet the man and gain further illumination. He received me and asked me to play him something of my own, but as I didn't have anything that was "playable", I sat down at the piano and improvised, as my grandfather would have done. 'Very Wagnerian', he said – and he was right because at that time I was re-discovering *Tristan* for myself, a work to which my father had introduced me perhaps too early and in too emotive a fashion. But the first book that I read on my own account was Romain Rolland's *Jean Christophe*. I read and re-read the ten volumes of that beautiful Beethovenian metaphor and I must say that *Jean Christophe* helped me to put my yearning for the sea behind me (I was just coming up to twelve at that crucial point). It is strange to remember all this now. But one result of provincial life (or of something else, who knows), is that I've always felt impelled to translate my inner experiences into concrete and practical terms. writing a "drama", setting off on a difficult journey, giving up the Idea of going to Naval Academy and a great number of other things both in and out of music. In short, I was a Bergsonian "homo faber" during those years and I didn't like to think that there might be a chasm between words and action.

D: Amongst all these experiences, one that you referred to earlier was La Bohème, *whose emotional impact you say that you soon got over. What did the discovery of* La Bohème *mean to you? A special moment, a revelation . . .?*

B: I was taken unawares by the emotional weight of the fourth act, and at that age I didn't know how to confront a phenomenon that was essentially physiological. But *La Bohème* is still very dear to me for musical reasons: Puccini came up with many new things in that opera.

D: Such as?

B: Puccini introduced the rhythm and the psychological mobility of everyday life into the musical theatre. He didn't articulate this through large-scale musical structures, but through a continually fragmented time-flow that nonetheless preserves its inner logic and unity. The time of the action and musical time are completely homogenous: the two levels are part of the same process. This is one of the reasons for the direct impact of Puccini – so that *La Bohème* offers one more solution to a perennial problem. Indeed, one of the most difficult and interesting (and least discussed) aspects of the musical theatre of all ages has been precisely this question of inventing temporal conventions that extend the relationship between words and dramatic action on one hand, and music on the other, making it flexible and dialectical. This search has always gone on under different names and pretexts. From tragedy to comedies with music, from "poetry handmaid of music" to "music handmaid of poetry", from intermezzos to the conventions of Italian melodrama, from the Wagnerian suspension of time to verismo, from cinematic cutting in *Wozzeck* to Stockhausen's spatio-temporal voyages into cosmic light. Puccini's experiment with time is very close to Debussy's, albeit using more rudimentary methods. Debussy effectively invented a new musical time, articulated through the repetition and continually transformed return of short elements that constantly change their function. They descend into the secondary regions, to the roots of the harmonic discourse and then emerge into new significance, following paths that seem to imitate the spontaneous mechanisms of mental association. The same thing, using more obvious and more elementary means, occurs for the first time in *La Bohème*, which is not merely the X-ray of a new moment in Italian music but is also a new musical reading of Puccini's contemporary world. After Puccini there was only "*puccinismo*". Puccini's only heir, and that a negative one, was Respighi whose operatic aspirations got more and more dessicated as he fattened out the Puccinian orchestra.

D: It's interesting that you should have noticed these things, even sub-consciously, at a time when Puccini was regarded above all as a purveyor of melodies.

B: No, at the time I was quite unable to recognize such things – apart from anything else I was too young.

D: All right, but the fact that you now rationalize your first encounter with Puccini in this way means that at the time he came across to you in a more intelligent way than, say, Mascagni.

B: Certainly. Mascagni was a troglodyte by comparison. I don't understand how Tuscany could have produced two such different operatic composers, born a few kilometres away from each other and a few years apart.

D: Everything that you have talked about so far has been concerned with, shall we say, the foundations of your career. But if we look more closely at the time when you started to write, would you now acknowledge a master, even if you had never met him personally – a particular source of sustenance, as it were?

B: Not easily, because I have an embarrassing ability to forget and to set things aside. Not out of ingratitude or lack of memory but as a matter of vocation: I usually work with my head down. Anyway, those musicians who personally gave me a great deal are Paribeni and Ghedini – while I was at the Conservatory – and subsequently Maderna and Pousseur. Ghedini was a great musician, but an uncomfortable and solitary man. I think that the history of Italian music will soon have need of him, and he will then be seen in a juster, and in some respects, a novel light. Some see the history of music as a series of problems that need solving, some try to contain it within a list of names and titles, some believe, even today, that the world of musical work and thought can coincide with power and wealth. And finally, some would hope to identify that world with the universe of human labour in general, where aspirations and transformations that aim towards real, not symbolic, improvements in life take on a concrete form. But it is a fact that, for better or for worse, the history of music, like any other history, chooses the right instruments and people at the right time (Beethoven and Schoenberg were well aware of this). So much so that you could say, without taint of determinism, that the course of history has a certain autonomy and continuity of its own, irrespective of names, titles, power, riches and the quality of life. History has a transcendence that leaves our relationship with the world unresolved. It's rather like a communication system possessing characteristics that function and evolve independently of the messages that it transmits and the people that use it. It's because of this that over relatively short periods history (and we, with it) can appear unfair, indifferent and forgetful. It can, for example, lose sight of important musicians who have contributed to music with very specific tasks. Or else it sometimes seems to have no need of very talented and intelligent young people, making them seem like abandoned or unexploited mines, because the mineral they contain does not have a visible and immediate application or, more simply, making them seem born in the wrong place at the wrong time.

These are not pessimistic observations, and it would certainly be unjust and far too dramatic to apply them to Ghedini, because the history that produced him is still with us and his work is still part of it. And anyway, we can't claim to know precisely how he will end up because history only really becomes clear to us when it is past and gone. I don't think that I am being blinded by gratitude for Ghedini as a teacher, if I say that I hope Ghedini the composer is quickly given the position that is due to him. After all, he was the first and only Italian musician to build a bridge of the highest quality, spanning two centuries of operatic paralysis, between the vocal and instrumental music of the Baroque and today. He was a very tormented, bitter and egoistic man. You couldn't label him: he wasn't part of the "Eighties generation", he wasn't "dodecaphonic", and he wasn't even likeable, like Malipiero. He wasn't a "character" either, but music was his extremely intelligent tool. His technique and his ear were infallible. I owe him so much, for example my first contact with Monteverdi. Not so much because, when Ghedini sat at the piano and sang Monteverdi it was an unforgettable experience, but because he could place Monteverdi within a very wide perspective: he could draw out of Monteverdi – in a very vivid and concrete way – three centuries of musical experience. His transcriptions of Monteverdi remain a mystery to me: I find them almost as embarrassing as Malipiero's. In Ghedini's class I always had the impression that there was a continuity between working with him and musical life outside the Conservatory, with its orchestral rehearsals, musicians passing through, technical problems, invectives, enthusiasms and (rather too much) gossip. Guido Cantelli, who had been a pupil of his, would often come to see him during classes, sometimes carrying a suitcase. Arriving from New York, he would stop off at the Conservatory even before he'd been home, and talk about his concerts with Toscanini's NBC orchestra. Ghedini, let me repeat, was a great musician even though he obstinately rejected the Viennese school, even though, cynically, he kept taking refuge in Verdi, and even though he was a man full of grudges, inexplicable envy and an excessive sarcasm.

D: And then there was Bruno Maderna

B: I first met Bruno in Milan in 1953 and we were friends from the first moment. It was the year in which I made my first pilgrimage to Darmstadt and when I also met Boulez, Stockhausen and Pousseur. I wouldn't know where to begin talking about Bruno and I doubt if I can do so in a way that is useful to other people. He is still too much part of me and it is still too difficult for me to separate my involvement in his private life from my involvement in his work. I was very close to him for a number of years: from 1953 to 1959 it was almost as if we were living together. So I know how much Bruno suffered. If anybody one day has the good fortune to read the letters that he wrote to Signora Manfredi of Verona, who had adopted him, they will have a better measure of Bruno's suffering, generosity, kindness, human awareness and essential fragility than any I could give. It isn't my business to do so now in any case. What I would like to do, though, is to convince editors and friendly musicians to collect together all of Bruno's works and to produce editions of them that don't too obviously bear the mark of everyday events and problems, of haste and of emergency solutions. For example, two of his masterpieces, *Hyperion* and *Aura* ought to be looked at again since his aleatoric solutions are rarely dictated by musical necessity. They need to be seen as sketches, annotations which were never set out in a more suitable way for lack of time. But the necessary materials are all there in specific and unambiguous form (as in the final part of *Aura*) and a solution could be found that didn't betray Bruno's intentions – and that indeed would clarify them. For he wasn't troubled by the drama of excessive organization becoming disorder, or by a desire to make the orchestra and conductor responsible for decisions which don't really affect the musical process in depth, but only the elementary, "de-synchronized" distribution of different elements. So everything possible should be done to make Maderna's music more accessible. All those little incongruities that are accidental and external to the substance of the music, and that put off many performers of little faith, should be eliminated.

D: And what of the general panorama of post-war musical life in Italy?

B: During those years I had formed a very close friendship, which continues to this day, with Henri Pousseur. Born a few kilometres from the German border, he succeeded in living within, and harmonizing in good Flemish fashion, two different cultures: the French and the German. But this takes us outside Italy where, in Milan, with Bruno and indirectly Nono, a circle of musical interests was forming based around the RAI's "*Studio di fonologia musicale*" and around the "*Incontri musicali*" concerts and journal. (I ended up paying for the greater part of the journal myself, with a loan of one million lira given me by my publisher Ladislao Sugar which it took me five years of hard work to pay back.) Musicologists such as Luigi Rognoni and Roberto Leydi, the philosopher Enzo Paci and Umberto Eco were all associated with us, as were many others, including those angry and elegant Leftists that Bruno named – with foresight and affectionate sarcasm – the "Vatican Hegelians". But between Ghedini on the one hand, and Maderna and Pousseur on the other, one other encounter was fundamentally important, not just for me, but for the whole of Italian music: Luigi Dallapiccola. In those years Dallapiccola was a point of reference that was not just musical, but also spiritual, moral and cultural in the broadest sense of the word. It was perhaps he, more than anyone else, who deliberately and unremittingly forged relationships with European musical culture. As often happens to me with important encounters, I reacted to Dallapiccola with four works: *Due pezzi*, for violin and piano, *Cinque variazioni*, for piano (based upon the three-note melodic cell – *"fratello"* – from *Il Prigioniero), Chamber Music* (setting poems by Joyce) and *Variazioni*, for chamber orchestra. With these pieces I entered into Dallapiccola's "melodic" world, but they also allowed me to escape from it. In 1952 I spent eight weeks with him in America at the Berkshire Music Center (Tanglewood), where he taught composition. Technically, he wasn't a good teacher, but neither Debussy, Ravel or Stravinsky would have been, had they taught.

D: I understand that he never really taught composition willingly. In Florence he taught score reading.

B: He too must have felt how difficult, if not impossible, it is to reduce a musical process to concepts. His nature being that of a true humanist, he would transfer musical experience to another level, a very broad one, and link it above all with literary experience. And he certainly knew how to appreciate things that he was obliged to forgo for musical reasons. In fact, his strict world of dodecaphonic melodies made his music rather impervious to the multiplicity of techniques and structures, and the associative epiphanies of, say, Joyce's work, to which he often liked to refer. After *Il Prigioniero,* his work is a determined, heroic hymn to canonic forms. This is part of the reason why the expressive world of his *Ulysses* is poles apart from that of Joyce: a granite stoicism, both spiritual and poetic, in the former, and a phantasmagoric entanglement of different forms, techniques and lexicons in the latter.

D: You met Dallapiccola in 1952 in the United States. Was this your first contact with American society?

B: I'd already been to the States in 1950, after Cathy Berberian and I had got married. My first contact with American society occurred in a taxi on the way from the liner to the hotel. The taxi driver, an Italian-American, asked me what I was doing in America, if I was staying permanently and how I made my living. I replied that I'd be staying in New York a few weeks, that I was a musician and that my job was writing music for chamber concerts and for symphony orchestras. He looked at me incredulously and said, "How do you make both ends meet with a job like that?"

The America of those years was perhaps more similar to the America of today than to that of ten or fifteen years ago – when the day of reckoning for the nation's ideals, culture and politics suddenly and movingly arrived. Then as now, anything which doesn't have a price and a market in America doesn't exist – or has no credibility, just as my job as a composer had no credibility for the Italian-American taxi driver. But I admit that this is an inevitable and paradoxical simplification, on a par with the American who says, "I don't like Italy because Italians are obsessed with food", or the wife of a friend who used to say, "I don't like America because the houses are all the same there". I'm no good at all when it comes to making generalized judgements about "Europeans", "Americans", "Orientals" or "Blacks". I simply mean that in America you can feel the presence of money as a social adhesive more strongly than elsewhere – defeating attempts at political and cultural renewal, because it casts a shadow of futility and uselessness over any possibility of renewal. I believe that the great scientific, technological and industrial innovations that are a constant feature of American life give an illusion of renewal, but that nothing really changes – even though these transformations impinge on a society that is culturally very richly heterogeneous. But I am also sure that if this is an opulent society, equipped with the most developed cultural tools (from the brains of academics in the big universities to the libraries, from a great literature to the symphony orchestras), it is at the expense of other people in other areas of the world.

Music doesn't escape the law of the market place. America, which is undoubtedly the most musical country in the world (in the sense that the majority of people have a direct and real contact with music making), has a very high standard of performance, a staggering number of orchestras – and an American orchestral musician earns in a week what his Italian equivalent earns in a month, with a more or less equal cost of living. Musical creativity doesn't escape the law of the market either. The most lively, authentic and interesting forms of American creativity are to be found in commercial music and, perhaps, in the really advanced research on music created with computers or synthesizers (linked to the electronics and computer industries). In the middle, between these two extremes – rock, pop, disco and jazz on the one hand, and "technological" and digital music on the other, (extremes which in America often overlap and influence each other on the level of pure *sound)* – there's the music of serious composers which naturally has no market. It lives inside academic citadels or else in the limbo of "foundations" that absorb and anaesthetize everything, even John Cage. In the United States the "serious" composer is materially well off, but his music is less fortunate, despite appearances. It is fairly often performed but has nobody to really address itself to, no cultural or spiritual destination, even sub-consciously. In other words, it lacks a real "market" of musical ideas that strive to represent a possible stage of being. It is fundamentally a music of solitude because, ironically, it lacks the vehicle of a market in a society where market value seems to be the necessary prerequisite for the recognition of anything at all, even the very things that the market inevitably destroys: human and cultural ideals. Nor is the American musical avant garde of much use – by now it seems a sort of mannerism. It pursues its debates within a society, in part like our own, where "the market trades in rejections of the market", in the words of Asor Rosa (one of the most useful thinkers in Italy today). Excluding Frederic Rzewsky, who is perhaps one of the most responsible and courageous composers in the United States (though he lives in Europe), I can't avoid a sense of inanity and alienation when I listen to the majority of young American composers – and indeed most of the others right back to Ives and that pseudo-American Varèse (whom I got to know well in his house on Sullivan Street, in the Village). Even if symphony orchestras include the music of these composers in the unvarying routine of their five weekly rehearsals, nothing really happens, nothing really changes and everything settles back to its previous state. Nor do the critics of the daily papers help very much: they are primarily interested in the technical quality of performance, and only rarely discuss the ideas implicit in one interpretation rather than another. I may be wrong, but the fact that the New York Philharmonic is a great orchestra has nothing to do with having had great conductors like Mahler, Bruno Walter, Mitropoulos, Bernstein and Boulez (who had to leave because his ideas didn't find an adequate market, so that subscriptions slumped). Even with a different past the New York Philharmonic would still be an extremely efficient, but forgetful musical machine. But here I'm simplifying again. America obviously provokes rather visceral reactions in me, perhaps because it is a country that I really do love very much, and which at the same time taxes me with rather complicated conflicts. I get bound up in its affairs as much as I do in Italy's. It's not for nothing that I spent many years of my life there.

INTERVIEW 3

with Rossana Dalmonte

D: Would you say that the musicians who started work at the beginning of the 1950's had a different character from those that preceded them, and shared things in common with each other?

B: Those features that musicians of my generation had in common were very deep-rooted but also very general: we were interested in the same things and we rejected broadly the same things. During the first years of the "Roaring Fifties" we shared a need to change, to clarify, to get a deeper knowledge of and to develop the serialist experience. Some felt the need to reject history, others who were more responsible wanted to re-read it and not accept anything without first examining it. Each one of us made a different contribution to an important evolution in music. I arrived at Darmstadt later than the others partly because I had difficulty in getting the necessary money together. In 1953 Stockhausen was the theoretical pivot of the *Ferienkurse*, Pousseur provided the speculative machinery, Boulez the analytical spirit and Maderna was a benign father-figure. Apart from the swarms of musical adventurers, the merchants of sonic carpets, junk, graphic extravaganzas, political gestures and musical cure-alls that made the Darmstadt *Ferienkurse* sometimes seem like a Bauhaus transplanted into a flea market, those years were, to say the least, fundamental. Boulez was turning his back on the combinatorial extremes which he had inherited from Messiaen and Cage, and which had acted as a catalyst without being either formative or, I would say, creative (the most notable and least satisfying results being Messiaen's, *Mode de valeurs et d'intensité*, and the first volume of Boulez's *Structures).* Stockhausen had written an indisputable masterpiece, *Kontrapunkte,* one of the real jewels of this period, and was using electronic music to pursue his quickly frustrated search for absolute unity of musical process and an identity between microstructure and macrostructure – which nowadays prompts him to look for a continuity between man and the biosphere and to make Teilhard de Chardin-like pronouncements. On the other hand, Bruno, with both feet firmly on the ground and an innate sense of history (he was never a disciplinarian or a visionary in his musical activities), gave an unselfconscious lesson in Humanism. It is mainly thanks to him that I approached serialist procedures (that is, the possibility of quantifying musical perception on the basis of proportions invented *ad hoc*), as a means of rediscovering and reorganizing things that were already familiar. It was Bruno, for example, who used overtly isorhythmic and therefore neutral criteria to experiment with taking conventional rhythmic modules, some of them with popular (especially Spanish) origins, and developing them so that sound and silence, rhythms and durations, formed an organic and inseparable unity whose relationship to the original popular models was indecipherable. Bruno had already passed on this approach to Nono, but apart from a few pieces that were written under his direct influence, Nono never really seemed to follow through their implications, unfortunately. In 1953, I wrote a "rumba" for my ballet *Allez-hop* based on Bruno's ideas, but at the time I needed a proper rumba, and not a sublimated one.

D: When did you move away from the central pre-occupations of Darmstadt?

B: My first reaction to Darmstadt and to Bruno's beneficial influence, in other words my first exorcism was *Nones* for orchestra which has nothing of Darmstadt or Maderna in it, but which develops what was for me the main focus of research and musical excitement during those years: the possibility of thinking musically in terms of process and not of form or procedure. André Souris and Pousseur were the theoretical champions of this tendency which was, in any case, implicit in the serial concept. My original project for *Nones* was very ambitious. These were the years in which I was discovering great English and American literature directly, rather than through Italian translations. I had fallen in love with a vast, complicated poem by Auden, *Nones:* the ninth hour, the crucial moment, the supreme moment in which all of existence seems to be conveyed in an instant, the moment of extreme awareness before the end. I had planned a great secular oratorio with solos, chorus and orchestra, characterized by constant, swift and extreme transformations. But the dimensions and the complexity of the poem dissuaded me, and I conserved from the uncompleted project only five orchestral episodes, five moments, five stages of transformation that, sewn together, form *Nones* for orchestra. Proportions based on nine, which predominate throughout, are constantly reorganized so as to produce extreme condensations or rarefications, extremes of speed and stasis, and extreme harmonic characteristics (from the octave to noise). I developed the experiences of *Nones* in *Allelujah*, which I immediately extended and developed in *Allelujah 11*. In these two pieces, expansive musical characteristics, an apparent "alleluiatic" disorder is kept at bay by hidden symmetries, by the cyclical return of continuously and statistically transformed structures that nevertheless retain "thematic" elements in common, such as the flute *b* flat that is the pivot, the starting point and the conclusion of every situation. I felt as if I was flying during those years. I knew I was getting to grips with new musical and acoustic dimensions that were opening up partly through my first experiences with electro-acoustics. During that period between 1953 and 1954, I really made up for all the time I'd lost in the provinces, especially during the war, and in Milan immediately after the war, when I took on any musical work I could get in order to make ends meet. My musical ear became more refined so that, for example, the orchestra stopped being the *orchestra*, that is, a historic arrangement of acoustic families, and became one whose relations could be re-examined on each occasion, in terms of the degree of fusion or of separation between them. During those years, through necessity, chance and *ça va sans dire*, because I wanted to, I carried out many practical experiments that were simple but useful, above all with Bruno Maderna. The *Studio di Fonologia Musicale* for electro-acoustic music was just starting up, and we threw ourselves body and soul into demonstrating the need for it, though without getting a penny out of the RAI – and as always, we were in great need of money. So we began writing music for any radio or television programme, for any director or any theatre that thought it wanted our music. We were always improvising together on the instruments that had been left unguarded in the studios in Corso Sempione, and I'd even gone to Paris to learn how to play the Ondes Martenot. But we also wrote ''functional'' scores together at an astronomical pace. Bruno, who was already putting on weight, would sit at my table and take care of the strings and the ''fixed sounds'' (which is what he called the guitar, piano, celesta and glockenspiel within the orchestra) and I, standing behind him, would take care of the wind instruments. We had reached such a stage of automatic understanding that each only needed to glance at what the other was writing to understand what he was aiming for. We were always late and I remember a copyist once watching horrified as we finished off a score composed in this way, by both of us at once. He left open-mouthed, with dilated eyes and hollow cheeks: he looked like a Giacometti statue. The point of this is that even in those moments of absolute musical cynicism we always found something to experiment with and, naturally, to learn from.

D: So even during the years of rigorous structuralism you didn't limit your own interests to that field.

B: It was during those years that I became interested, at first intuitively, in expressing a continuity between different realities, even if they were very distant from each other and sometimes even trivial. As far as I was concerned, the serial experience never represented the utopia of a language, and so it could never be reduced to a norm or to a restricted combination of materials. What it meant for me above all was an objective enlargement of musical means, the chance to control a larger musical terrain (such as the ethnic materials that I have often worked with) while respecting, indeed admiring, its premises. Bruno basically shared the same attitude even though he realized his musical visions in a different way and with expressive characteristics that were perhaps the opposite of mine. This interest in exploring the continuity of musical processes – even in the morphology of their sound-materials – explains why the pieces that affected me most during those years, and about which I was most enthusiastic, constituted a fairly heterogeneous group: Stockhausen's *Gesang der Jünglinge*, Maderna's *Serenata*, and later on, Pousseur's *Rimes*, and *Agon* by Stravinsky. *Agon* is a triumph not only of invention and, in its own way, of awareness and of courage, but also of the transformation of materials. Onto a subcutaneous tissue (as Schoenberg would have called it) that is, a harmonic structure that glides from *G* major to a Webernian series (and back again) through various stages of chromatic corruption, there unfolds in remorseless, exemplary and naive fashion, the hyper-intelligent parable of a "short history of music" that performs a lucid, but tragic autopsy on itself under the pretext of a game. It is so difficult to hear it well performed.

D: But there is one aspect of the serial experience of those years that has preserved, indeed developed, very deep roots in you.

B: You're thinking of my short-lived adoption of those rigorous and abstract combinatorial processes that the Americans call pre-composition – for example, the famous "magic squares" that Bruno used in his *Quartetto per archi*, as I also did in a rather desultory way in my *Serenata* – essentially arbitrary and only weakly directional conglomerations that were then filtered by selective rhythmic models (Maderna's and Nono's Spanish rhythms for instance) and by durational proportions. It was really a question of extracting musical functions and specific musical characteristics from what was essentially a statistical distribution of elements. As I was saying, the filter could be a series of durations, but it could also be a series of intervals, a sequence of notes, of intensities of instrumental colours etc; in other words, anything that could be symbolically quantified . . . There was the danger in all this of a certain abstractness or excessive interchangeability between acoustic parameters, which were usually reduced to numerical symbols. For example, proportion between durations could act as a filter for a group of frequencies, and these in turn could filter dynamic values, and so on. By now these procedures belong among the serialist anecdotes of those years, (though they were more subtle and flexible than those adopted by Boulez in his *Structures 1*). Even so, they contained the seed of something fundamentally important – something that I believe to be "universal" whose nature continues even now to condition my musical conduct. There's no doubt that we always carry around with us our precedents – a mass of experiences, "the mud on our shoulders", as Sanguineti put it, and therefore a virtual set of choices from the perennially present noise of history. And we can filter that noise, responsibly and consciously selecting one thing rather than another – and trying to understand which combination of the selected and filtered events corresponds best to our needs, and allows us to give a better account of ourselves. This is true for musical processes and functions, as it is for any others.

D: So in practice there is no such thing as the degré zéro de la musique.

B: No, there can be no *tabula rasa,* especially in music. But this tendency to work with history, drawing out and consciously transforming historical "minerals", and absorbing them into musical materials and processes that don't bear the mark of history, reflects a need – that has been with me for a long time – to organically continue a variety of musical experiences, and thus to incorporate within the musical development different degrees of familiarity, and to expand its expressive design and the levels on which it can be perceived. Excuse this rather cryptic and equivocal language, but I am talking about something that is so deeply rooted in me that I don't know where to begin. . . Anyway, in 1976, I took a step forward in my research with *Coro*. With the many encounters and identifications that take place in it, it's a bit like a huge musical metaphor for a ballad. It's also my Jerusalem: a city whose marvellously beautiful white stones have been used across the centuries for different things, but are reunited in new buildings, with new functions, under different religions and different administrations . . . This tendency to embrace a totality – always implicitly present but always "filtered" – is not just a form of musical behaviour like any other, but a way of thinking, and thus of being, that exists irrespective of any historical and cultural references that it may propose. I'd say that, for me, it's a sort of archetypal structure. I don't think there's anything that represents this tendency better for me than Beethoven's sketch books: this totality that unveils the formation of a musical process, that reduces and defines itself little by little through filtering and selection on the one hand, and through amplification and deeper exploration on the other. The successive stages in Beethoven's creative process hardly ever suggest a linear route, a discourse that is constructed and perceived "from left to right". If anything, they suggest a total, summated event that sinks into us without any before and after – as if the need for a before and an after were a quite secondary and trivial convention. The idea that in Beethoven everything points towards the end, an end that then doesn't want to end and repeats over and over again, is a mystification stemming from the serialist distaste for rhetoric. There are pieces by Beethoven, those that I think I know particularly well and to which I feel very close, that I perceive and "feel" globally, without a beginning and an end, like an organic, non-chronological whole, or a huge process of mutation. I am thinking for example of that ineffable and somewhat labyrinthine meditation, the "Adagio" from Op. 106 (where, amongst other things, there's a glimpse of Chopin in a quite clear *ante litteram* citation). The fact is that with Beethoven, the great gesture, the great process, the great musical event (whether it be the *Third* or *Fourth Symphony, Fourth Piano Concerto,* Op. 106, 111, 135, etc.) seems to emerge every time, dripping with precedents, from a totality that contained that great process, and from which Beethoven, like Michelangelo, has hacked it out "*a forza di levare*". We thus have a totality that "speaks" the piece, and to which the piece continually alludes through innumerable, and disconcerting ways. And here we are naturally at the opposite pole from the general principles of Webernian serialist practice. Principles that were, essentially, of an additive and conventional nature: an embryo, a three-note cell that is projected, as if within a transparent prism, into all the interstices of the piece. It was this idea that was among other things the starting point for the experience of electronic music, but that also, within that perspective, defined its limits.

D: You referred previously to Bruno Maderna's Quartetto per archi, *one of his most significant pieces. In that piece, it seems to me that there is already something of what you were saying about the tendency to adopt subtractive criteria.*

B: I'm pleased that you noticed it. The *Quartetto* is in two parts. The first, in all its aspects, is the product of a strict combinatorial procedure; the second part is a retrograde reading of the first. But on the quantitative level it's an improverishing reading, one that filters, eliminates, introduces spaces, and thus reorganizes the time-span and the material that have just been heard on a different level, a level of the highest expressive quality. I don't know if we'll talk about Bruno again, but with regard to his *Quartetto* I'd really like to dedicate to him a famous axiom by Jacques Monod, who loved and cultivated music as much as biology: "Selection acts upon the products of chance; however, it operates within a field of rigorous necessities from which chance is banished". I wouldn't attempt to establish a relation between the biologist's "chance" and "chance" in the first part of Bruno's *Quartetto;* but there is a relation between the different "fields of rigorous necessities" to be found in both vital processes and creative processes.

As everybody knows, one of the most important and symptomatic aspects of the serialist experience was the separation of musical "parameters" ideally comparable (though not in its practical consequences) with the separation of dramaturgical "parameters" in Brecht's theatrical work. A sort of *divide et impera* in other words. When this dividing up of "parameters" was applied scholastically, for analytical purposes, to musical pieces where the solidarity between intervals, durations, instrumental timbre, intensity and register was organically implicit in the expressive and structural design of the piece, then the operation had, and still has, a meaning. It was rather like examining the separate pieces of a motor while knowing that the elementary sum of these parts didn't constitute the motor (our perception always plays such tricks on us). The problems started when, inevitably, people began going in the opposite direction, taking unattached pieces, separate "parameters", and putting them together under the indifferent and uniform light of abstract proportions, and then waiting for the unveiling of the piece (or the non-piece – which is after all the same thing because, as you know, by night all cats are grey).

This tendency, which derives in large part from Webern's last works, has had its heroic, and also its comic-heroic moments. Amongst other things, it's helped to institute a certain indifference between material and form, and to suggest that an inert, "functional" material, devoid of creative necessity, is worth just as much as material enriched by musical experiences and intentions. Obviously, here we are in the aleatoric sphere, but in a modest form of it where every higher form of selection becomes superfluous, and where exegetes of the avant garde use incoherent verbal acrobatics to demonstrate a direct link between the highly organized discharge of notes in a Pousseur *Mobile* and Paik trying to cut off an outraged spectator's tie. That indifference between material and form – implicit, as I said, in the final offshoots of serialism – finally broke down into a total absence of relationship between the conceptual and the physical, between project and result. This produced a sort of meta-aleatoricism, which focussed maximum attention on raw acoustic materials, isolating them from the conceptual procedures (whether "true" or "false") by which they had been organized (and which have to be there anyway, because human action is never free of concepts). The conceptual aspect, left in isolation and reduced to an abstraction that had no need of concrete relations, was much discussed, but in the end it was the physical materials that took over. And when objects took over from thought, they produced a string of gratuitous and renunciatory gestures. That was what happened with those experiences that proposed to let "things themselves" sound and speak, as if there were no difference between perception and understanding, sensation and thought, listening to the sound of water, and listening to *Götterdämmerung*. The ultimate example of this was the thoroughly stupid gesture of the pianist in evening dress circulating round the piano without playing it, as if his refusal to do so hid some greater ontological refusal in the background. When the conceptual and the physical aspects of music propose themselves as separate and irreconcilable entities, I have the impression that I'm listening to someone who reminds us continually of his vocabulary, his syntax and his figures of speech (though in fact he shouldn't need the latter), but conceals from us whatever message he may have to transmit. With the difference, though, that the man who talks may at least amuse us because, in unconscious parody, he mimes certain of the essential ingredients of poetic discourse, whereas the producer of free sounds and noises ends up depicting the post-Cagean squalor of his soul and his musical intellect, and nothing more.

D: Is this not more an American phenomenon than a European one?

B: Often, especially in America, the need to separate out the conceptual and physical aspects, and to point out their independence on an elementary level of activity, conceals a reductive attitude borrowed in part from the art market.

In fact, there are musicians who, like certain painters that are enslaved by their dealers, have to be heroically and indefatigably faithful to themselves. They have to perpetuate the attitudes and gestures that gained them the first successes of their career. If they don't, they lose their identity, their market and, naturally, their all too vulnerable position within the crowded ranks of the avant garde. I get the impression that behind the far-from-desperate musical folly of a Morton Feldman who writes everything pianissimo, lies the fear of taking even a step out of the "avant garde", lest he should unintentionally land up in those regions which in old maps used to carry the inscription "*hic sunt leones*",

where music opens out with all its volcanoes, its seas and its hills.
Maybe he is afraid of being eaten alive.

INTERVIEW 4

with Rossana Dalmonte

D: You've taught a good deal in the United States, at Tanglewood, San Francisco, Cambridge and New York. Would you say the same thing about yourself as you said about Dallapiccola, that is, that you're a bad teacher?

B: The number of young people who have worked with me in one way or another, particularly at the Juilliard School, is enormous, so it shouldn't be difficult to find one and put that question to him. Perhaps his answer would be more predictable than mine. I stopped teaching in 1972 because I could no longer commit myself to being on duty twice a week. And anyway, there were too many students. Apart from the seminars, which I always enjoyed giving, what was so tiring was the individual lessons: the students expected me at specific times and I saw them one after another every half hour. So-and-so at nine o'clock, so-and-so at nine-thirty: I thought I'd turned into a dentist.

D: Do you think it's possible to teach composition?

B: I think that once a certain basis has been established, a young composer has to carry on by himself and hunt out the things that he needs. As far as I'm concerned, that basis is first counterpoint, and then analysis. Not that I'm nostalgic for the great days of counterpoint, but I don't yet know of any other means of getting a student to train himself systematically in linking up his brain and his ears. There's no need to be too finicky about this: any type of counterpoint will do, provided it's being taught by a responsible teacher and is placed coherently within its historical and technical context: the Burgundians, Palestrina, Bach, Fux, Cherubini and, why not, Dubois. The pupil must of course be young, must be steered away from making an ideology out of counterpoint, and must learn it as he would the rules of a game. In other words, you've got to make sure that, later on, this experience of counterpoint doesn't transform itself into a regressive refuge, a reactionary technical instrument. When a boy can write a four or five part fugue in half a day without the help of a piano, at least you can be certain that he'll be a good artisan – which is something that the world has desperate need of these days. But there's something else that is perhaps not the concern of composition teaching, but of the teaching of music in general. I don't think that with children of between three and ten years old you can start differentiating between types of musical education: with one for those who are more than likely to take up a musical profession, and another for those who are not. In fact I think that the simplest forms of counterpoint (to be made up in class and then sung) could be a very useful common starting point, and certainly a more natural, and therefore a more egalitarian one than chords on the various degrees of the scale. A young person must be given the means to read and assimilate a great deal of music and, if he plays an instrument, must be encouraged to put his brain between his eyes and his fingers. I don't believe in authoritarian teaching, but I do believe in discipline. And I don't believe in being self-taught either. I'm always suspicious of those who label themselves in this way: it usually means that their technical capacities are fragile. Anyway, I find it difficult to imagine a young person these days actually wanting to be self-taught; that sort of situation might be imposed on him (by lack of money, absence of teachers etc.) but he'd hardly choose it for himself. How can anyone not want to learn from other people within a modestly systematic framework? Perhaps self-taught people are basically rather weak and shy away from measuring themselves up against someone who is necessarily "better at it" than they are, in other words the teacher. Or perhaps they restrict their relations with music to a set of private and personal games. There's the case of Schoenberg who said he was self-taught, but in fact was nothing of the sort: he started learning the violin when he was eight years old, was enveloped in music and the other arts even when he was working in a bank and then, when he was nineteen, found an ideal tutor in Zemlinsky . . . And anyway,

Schoenberg was the sort of man who would have moved mountains to respond to the call: in fact that's exactly what he did. Perhaps the only place where Schoenberg reveals a self-taught temperament is in his *Harmonielehre*, where he exalts that most typical defect of the self-taught: the constant discovery and rediscovery of the most obvious facts. It's the extraordinary context in which these discoveries are made that makes the book into a fundamental, and justly famous work. It's a profound, dramatic, and at the same time pathetic document that echoes almost obsessively through many other, later writings by Schoenberg. Not for nothing did he subsequently revise and "correct" it. I see the *Harmonielehre* as a desperate attempt to give rational justification to a harmony that was breaking up on all sides, undertaken by one of those primarily responsible for that harmonic break-up. But I wouldn't recommend the book, which was, after all, written by a man sailing in deep water, for teaching purposes: it's much too prescriptive, verbose, repetitious and lacking in any real synthesis. Though you will find that synthesis in later writings of his, or in the *ex cathedra* remarks that you come across every so often in the *Harmonielehre* itself. The fact that Schoenberg tended to overvalue the harmonic dimension as such, to functionalize and formalize it in scholastic fashion as an independent musical dimension – thus echoing Schenker despite himself – just at the moment when he was himself creating music in which all musical dimensions (with the partial exception of rhythm) were short-circuiting, might lead one to think that the *Harmonielehre* acted as a sort of psychological life-line for him. Something like what writing *Les mots anglais* may have been for Mallarmé.

Be that as it may, in composition teaching – as in any other form of teaching – there have to be points of reference in common between teacher and pupil. They have to understand one another with regard to concrete aspects of musicial experience, and to engage on these rather than on generic speculations. Once the instrument was the vehicle of thought; it's worth recalling that one of Beethoven's reasons for going to Vienna – if I'm not mistaken – was that he hoped to study with Mozart, whose way of playing had made such a deep impression on him. Nowadays the instrument can no longer offer a meeting-point (if it could, it would indicate a rather happy-go-lucky attitude): what can take its place, though, is a continuous, extended and unstinting exercise in "writing" and analysis. When you're young, it's not enough to know how to write a fugue (or whatever else it may be); you have to write lots and lots of them. I firmly believe that a student must be able to see through to completion a large amount of work (why not think of "inspiration" as an organ that needs to be exercised?), and that quantity as such is indispensible if you want to consolidate a significant and dialectical, that is, useful unity between practice and intellectual speculation, between concrete and abstract. It's not an easy thing to do. I'm sure that without that *quantity* you can't achieve evolutions or transform-ations, let alone revolutions: in the end, as Asor Rosa reminds us, "liberty, equality and fraternity are nothing without the guillotine" . . . and perhaps it's no accident that the first guillotine was constructed by a piano-maker.

D: What do you think are the most interesting tendencies today amongst younger composers?

B: As I said before when I was talking about Ghedini, it seems to me that history is rather ungenerous with today's younger composers, and sometimes I have the impression that it has no need of them. To put it in a rather intolerant and authoritarian way, you might say that they themselves have been intolerant and ungenerous with history, so history is getting its own back. Anyway, I don't mean history in general, nor a particular history but rather the sense of our position in history and the sense of the history of things. The crisis that we hear so much discussed also means, I suppose, a crisis in our sense of history. There are currently so many tendencies in the music of the young that I wouldn't know where to begin describing them. Nor am I the best person to do it. You'd need to buy in your labels wholesale: there are such a lot of current tendencies that I wonder if it wouldn't be better to call them mannerisms. Something is missing deep down in the consciousness of a number of young people which can, on the other hand, be found in anyone with a sense of history. Thus alongside the enthusiasm for a pluralistic and centrifugal musical world, almost all of which remains to be charted, analyzed and dominated, there ought to be acknowledgement of the elementary fact that musical languages also have to be transmitted, and a utopian vision of a common language that will allow music and musicians to speak and to be universally spoken. Without this covertly implied and perhaps unrealizable ideal, music cannot move, loses one of its dialectical reasons for existing and drifts from one mannerism to the next. It's useful to search for things that we know we can't find . . .

D: Does anything seem to stand out particularly within this multitude of languages, as far as you're concerned?

B: Among the many current tendencies and mannerisms there's one that strikes me as rather curious and pathetic: the reconquest of melody. Nowadays my friend Pousseur preaches that we must snatch melodies from the enemy, and then use them against him. *Ergo,* we should be producing melodies governed by progressive criteria and getting the "workers" to sing them in order that they may liberate themselves from the melodic power of the bosses. The results are dreary and senseless tunes that nobody sings, and that take no account of a fact of primary importance: as I pointed out to Pousseur myself, the processes that generate melody cannot be manufactured from one day to the next – melodies are born spontaneously within collective groups or in a stylistic frame when all the "parameters" of music are at peace, and start "singing" together. Anyway, it seems to me that there is a political error of some substance within this preconceived search for "popular" melody, conceived as something to make and use rather than as the result, and not necessarily a spontaneous one, of a process of collective sedimentation. Let's assume that the error is simply this: the working class, the lower and upper middle classes and the economic powers that be must, in one way or another, go along the same road together, and so they often sing the same tunes, from *Bella Ciao* to the Beatles. Since we know that bankers don't produce melodies though agricultural labourers do, and that melody is a meeting-point, albeit a superficial and emotive one, for socio-cultural classes in open or latent conflict, all we can really do is study the processes that govern the making of melodies (more than a life-time's work in itself), and wait for the emergence of easy and singable melodies that will certainly contribute to the resurgence of the oppressed classes in a better world ... I'm joking, of course; but one of the reasons why this search for melodies *à tout prix* awakens violent reactions in me is that it reminds me of Hans Eisler – whose example Pousseur acknowledges, but with whom he has nothing in common, being a much better musician all round. Eisler manufactured melodies for the workers and every so often, the better to round out and "realize" himself, he also wrote chamber music "à la Schoenberg", just as you might make a wardrobe "à la Mondrian" or write a little song "à la Brahms". The two worlds, if you can call them that, had nothing whatever to do with each other, and like the fine but rather schizophrenic entrepreneur that he was, Eisler often sought to justify their contiguity with the conceited arrogance of someone so caught up in the means of production that he no longer even bothered about the quality of the product, which descended to unspeakable levels, but only about the political message that it was to transmit (which was in any case crudely Stalinist-Zdanovian). It's no surprise that one of Eisler's most peculiar characteristics was the total distrust that he had of the cognitive and expressive powers of music; not only, understandably, in the cognitive powers of his own "stupid" music but also, among many others, that of Mozart ... In fact, it was he who wrote that poor Mozart had no culture and was unaware of his enlightened contemporaries because from his earliest youth he had studied only music, and had been able to learn nothing else. In other words, for Eisler Mozart was a good musician with a half-empty head. This tendency to deny music's autonomy and intellectual authority, and thus to imply that human thought, in its highest and richest forms, cannot be expressed musically casts its shadow even now over certain areas of musicology and music criticism. The only text of Eisler's that has a certain coherence and solidity is the one on film-music – but as everyone knows, that was written in collaboration with Adorno. Anyway, it's clear enough that Eisler's melodies have been no use to anyone. Not even to Brecht, when all is said and done: in Brecht choices are made primarily within the theatrical process whereas in Eisler choices are always made outside the musical process. With different words, Eisler's songs could have been used by Hitler, and he'd have enjoyed every minute of them, even though Eisler's name appeared in that famous pamphlet on "degenerate art" (Kurt Weill's name was there too, but Hitler would never have been able to use his tunes). Eisler's music was essentially stupid (it's a word that he often used himself), and therefore its cognitive power was nil: it wasn't even an effective political instrument, just populist demagogy.

D: There is, or at least there was, another trend amongst the young: improvisation.

B: There were a lot of different motives behind this trend, not all of them equally respectable: a desire to refashion the unity between musical creation and performance, the tendency to push to extreme and spectacular forms the aleatoric approach, the search for a new type of interaction between musicians, parody, satire, meditation, exhibitionism, etc. Rare, fleeting moments of interest apart (when the musicians involved were of considerable quality), improvisation has been a haven for dilettantes, who may be fluent in inventing socio-musical alibis but are in most cases quite incapable of evaluating and analyzing themselves in relation to any historico-musical perspective. Improvisation during the baroque era was somewhat like jazz improvisation in that it based itself upon a harmonic (and therefore a rhythmic and metric) structure that was clear and, as it were, unanimous. Nowadays improvisation presents a problem: above all because there's no true unanimity of discourse among the participants, only, once in a while, a unanimity of behaviour. The real problem of improvisation as compared to written composition is that improvisation segments musical space in a different, and cruder way. At best, it tends towards a segmentation into "syllables" and not, like written music, into "phonemes": in other words, into primary units of a psychomotoric nature rather than into derived and evolutive units. The improviser is rather like someone who, while observing the animal world, apes for instance, only manages to sort out gorillas from chimpanzees, whereas when you write music down (having thought first), it's like managing to segment that world with greater finesse, distinguishing all its possible species and subspecies including, of course, King Kong and Tarzan's stepmother. Improvisation – nowadays, in our own culture – is a sort of private experience which doesn't belong in a public place such as a concert hall – even though it is precisely this context at which improvisational activities are often aimed. In fact, whenever I have heard improvisations in the concert hall – whether in Rome, Paris or New York – I have always felt slightly uncomfortable, as if I'd walked through the wrong door and was now obliged to watch some fine people, perhaps a little mad, on the point of doing something very private that concerned nobody but themselves. I really don't believe that a "serious" musician improvising in a concert hall can articulate a discourse of a complexity and interest comparable to that of a baroque musician or even a jazz musician. Baroque improvisation was composition that hadn't been written down, and there was no substantial difference between what Bach wrote *for* and what he improvised *on* the harpsichord. In baroque improvisation, written music was implicitly present, as was a continuously controlling *eye*. Even today, of all the things that can happen when improvising, it seems to me that it's those elements which establish a relation with a more or less explicit idea of notation that make sense – even if it is an antagonistic relation: improvisation as the manifestation of an elementary impulse towards liberation, a desire to separate expression from form, if I can put it that way. And in general it's only the specific characteristics of performing technique that have power to suggest references to written music. The marginal and desultory interest that improvisation is currently capable of stimulating derives principally from those flashes of instrumental inspiration that may subsequently open the way to moderately interesting discoveries in instrumental technique, and thus be assimilated into musical thought. Even the improvisations of really well-integrated groups that bring together the very best instrumentalists, such as New Phonic Art, always have a private character to them, precisely because they cannot, as improvisers, place themselves within a sufficiently wide and objective dimension of musical experience. I know all the New Phonic Art players well, and they're all good friends of mine; indeed, two of them were pupils of mine – and I admire them a great deal. But when I see Vinko Globokar, Michel Portal, Carlos Roqué-Alsina and Jean-Pierre Drouet doing extravagant things on stage, producing exhilarating actions and unusual sounds, none of which they do normally, I can't help feeling that these things conserve a semblance of meaning for me only if I can relate them to their author's musical concerns and personal musical history, to the authors themselves as friends of mine – and also, of course, to the "normal" sound and use of their respective instruments. The same sort of thing happens to me in John Cage's "concerts": if he's not on stage I get horribly bored. Anyhow, improvisation usually acts on the level of instrumental praxis rather than musical thought. Globokar, particularly, has sometimes tried to transfer the experience of improvisation into written music, and with attractive results, too. But I don't believe that musical thought needs improvisation to develop itself, to manifest itself in finished form, and to make itself useful to other people in one way or another. What it needs is a more stable and selective medium. Jazz improvisation is another matter, because it is based on the rapid extraction of musical modules and instrumental gestures from the great reservoir of memory, and it is also based on speed of reaction to one's partners and to oneself – it's somewhat similar to the rapid reflexes involved in the act of speech. Perhaps you could also consider jazz improvisation as a continuous correction of little errors, a continuous adjusting of sights relative to a target that, by its very nature, is never perfectly clear and defined. It's significant that the pianist Thelonious Monk, unhappy with an improvisation that he had just finished, walked out with the splendid remark "I made the wrong mistakes".

Still, on a very personal level "highbrow" improvisation can have some "therapeutic" value. For example, it can help a musician to get rid of some of his complexes, and gain a better knowledge of himself by relating to intuitive materials. Which is not to say that you can't sometimes get some fairly astonishing things happening on the levels of *time*, technique, and instrumental anecdote: it's just that nothing interesting ever happens, even by chance, on the level of musical thought. And by musical thought I mean above all the discovery of a coherent discourse that unfolds and develops simultaneously on different levels.

There's also an aspect of the improvisatory experience that belongs to the realm of ideals: a para-political aspect, I'm tempted to say, which can make New Phonic Art appear not only as a small group of superb musicians but also as a little commando group of musical guerillas who infiltrate enemy lines to shake up the subscription holders and incite revolt amongst the young. But 1968 was a long time ago, and improvisation can provoke neither revolutions nor crises of conscience, above all when it is (or was) those same subscribers who invite and pay the improvisers. Even so, it was good to watch the tacit but deep understanding that linked the members of New Phonic Art when they were all working together on stage. and it was sometimes interesting to observe the collective transformation of something (a sound, a gesture, an attitude), to follow the ups and downs of an intuitive process being played out in front of you, *hic et nunc*, and to try and involve yourself in perceiving that process. From this point of view, as a sharpener of the spirit, improvisation could provide a useful tool for re-educating our friends the subscribers, or indeed anyone who has settled too comfortably into a musical routine... But in the end all this is rather abstract because the "language" of improvisation doesn't really open up pedagogical paths: usually the significant elements, whether internalized or externalized, that should be the starting-point for an improvisation and should be involved in a process of transformation, can't be recognized, so that sometimes you begin to wonder whether they are there at all. . . .

INTERVIEW 5

with Rossana Dalmonte

D: Perhaps we should now move into your 'workshop'. How much do you know about one of your works when you begin writing it? How much do you stick to the original idea as you set it down?

B: The first idea of a work is always global and very general for me, as it is for everybody, I think. Then I define the details. But I don't believe that "first" ideas exist; and anyway, in the course of defining the details, I may discover new possibilities over which I decide to linger, though that doesn't change the nature or the motive of the project. It's a bit like deciding to go on a journey, say to China. An idea of this sort can't suddenly appear out of nowhere, and it's not as if there was only one way of getting there. If the journey hasn't been arranged beforehand in Peking by a group of bureaucrats, and I'm free to go there as I please, then the journey can become a source of interesting discoveries. On the way I can decide to stay in one place longer than I had envisaged and I might even plan to return there by a completely different route. And then, absurd as it may sound, I'll walk home from China or at most cycle back. I don't want to miss the details of the countryside and the cities that I'd flown over on the way out. I don't like stochastic journeys which pay attention only to the general form, the wrapping, but not to the concrete relations that may responsibly be realized within it. In the same way I don't like architects who become set designers: they come up with a good design, give it to the theatre, and impatiently wait for those poor people in the scenographic workshop to make it up. And I don't like architecture that lacks precise functions and doesn't respect the life, the ideals and the work of ordinary people. I prefer a Park Avenue skyscraper that is free from ideals, not too free, though, to the Pyramids of Egypt. In the course of realizing a global project and defining its details, as I was saying earlier, it may happen that the discovery and proliferation of unforeseen elements becomes so important that it effectively alters the project. When this happens I follow the opposite path: from the details that I had worked out and put together I move on to a different project. Like a good Ligurian, I never throw anything away. This is what links *Allelujah* to *Allelujah II*, *Sequenza II* to *Chemins I*, *Sequenza VI* to *Chemins II* and *III*, *Sequenza VII* to *Chemins IV*, *Sequenza VIII* to *Corale* or else, moving in the opposite direction, *Chemins V* to *Sequenza IX*.

D: Are long-standing projects like your Sequenzas *(where there are about twenty-two years between the first for flute and the latest for clarinet) part of a plan, or do they come into being by chance?*

B: My first *Sequenza* for flute was composed in 1958 for Severino Gazzelloni, and it was certainly no chance that we were both going to Darmstadt at the time. Meeting up with the harp of Francis Pierre was no accident either, and my encounter with the voice of Cathy Berberian even less so. In the *Sequenzas* as a whole there are various unifying elements, some planned, others not. The most obvious and external one is virtuosity. I hold a great respect for virtuosity even if this word may provoke derisive smiles and even conjure up the picture of an elegant and rather diaphanous man with agile fingers and an empty head. Virtuosity often arises out of a conflict, a tension between the musical idea and the instrument, between concept and musical substance. The most obvious and elementary example in painting occurs when an artist uses oil paints and brushes to produce a painting that looks like a photograph. In music things are more complicated because there's the familiar problem of performance and re-interpretation ... As is well-known, virtuosity can come to the fore when a concern for technique and stereotyped instrumental gestures gets the better of the idea, as in Paganini's work – which I'm very fond of, but which didn't really shake up the history of music, although it did contribute to the development of violin technique. Another instance where tension arises is when the novelty and the complexity of musical thought – with its equally complex and diverse expressive dimensions – imposes changes in the relationship with the instrument, often necessitating a novel technical solution (as in Bach's *Violin Partitas,* Beethoven's last piano works, Debussy, Stravinsky, Boulez, Stockhausen, etc.), where the interpreter is required to perform at an extremely high level of technical and intellectual virtuosity. Finally, as I've often emphasized, anyone worth calling a virtuoso these days has to be a musician capable of moving within a broad historical perspective and of resolving the tension between the creativity of yesterday and today. My own *Sequenzas* are always written with this sort of interpreter in mind, whose virtuosity is, above all, a virtuosity of knowledge. (I've got no interest in, or patience for those who "specialize" in contemporary music.) Another unifying element in the *Sequenzas* is my own awareness that musical instruments can't really be changed, destroyed or invented. It is not only those occasional conflicts between idea and executive technique that are responsible for the slow transformation of instruments across the centuries, but also evolutions in the economic and social structure of the public. It would be, to say the least, naive to suggest that Beethoven, in his last piano works, effectively *invented* the modern piano without taking into account the place that these deeply impressive pieces had in a world where music, in search of bigger spaces and audiences, was in any case becoming louder and more "noisy". It was only when *everybody* wanted a more resonant piano, that the manufacturers replaced the wood inside the instrument with steel. In the end, the sale of musical instruments – and their manufacture – is subject to the same market forces as any other consumer goods that are industrially produced. I think it's very important to understand – which is why I'm insistent about it – that a musical instrument is in itself a piece of musical language. To try and invent a new one would be as futile and pathetic as trying to invent a new grammatical rule for our language. The composer can only contribute to the transformation of musical instruments by using them, and trying to understand *post factum* the complex nature of the transformations. The individual is partially excluded from the logic and continuity of the transform-ations. A bit like a transport system where the continuity and the ways in which it changes stem from the system itself rather than from the traveller. No one has ever been able to change the violin. After 350 years it is still the same – if you exclude the bow and its technique and what the strings are made of, all of them things that have helped to increase its carrying power. I am very much attracted by this slow and dignified transformation of instruments and techniques across the centuries. This is perhaps why, in all of my *Sequenzas*, I have never tried to alter the nature of the instrument, nor to use it "against" its own nature. In fact, I have never been able to insert screws and rubbers between the strings of a piano, nor even to attach a contact microphone to a violin, although I am totally committed to extending instrumental performance by using new digital techniques. At IRCAM over the past few years, some musicians have been trying to change and "improve" the flute: they have moved the holes and given it different keys, and indeed, once it has been manipulated in this way, the flute is able to produce chords and some very unusual effects. But the wretches have had to forget about Bach, Mozart, Debussy and even my *Sequenza*. They couldn't even play a scale of C major in tune any more. Quite a loss, when all is said and done if, as Adorno so rightly said, techniques are also an instrument of socialization. It may well be due to my "eurocentricity", but I always thought that to "prepare" a piano was a bit like drawing a moustache on the Mona Lisa, even when the pretext was to explore a non-tempered musical space. I ask myself why such a well-tempered instrument was ever chosen: it must be because there are lots of pianos everywhere, and they are virtually indestructible – and then one can always find a pianist who is prepared to decipher Cage's old fly-papers. It makes no difference, the piano has remained the same, and it has certainly survived being violated by kind and smiling Americans.

D: Could you describe one of your Sequenzas *in more detail?*

B: In my *Sequenzas* I have often tried to develop specific technical aspects of the instrument in greater depth, and sometimes I have also tried to develop a musical commentary between the virtuoso and his instrument by disassociating various types of behaviour and then putting them together again, transformed, as musical unities. This is the case, for example, in *Sequenza III* for voice, written for Cathy Berberian, and *Sequenza V* for trombone, written for Stuart Dempster, both of which, because of this process of disassociation, can also be experienced as dramatic entities. In *Sequenza V* the theatrical element is explicit because the piece makes open reference to the great clown Grock and, in particular, to his famous, metaphysical *"warum" (Sequenza V* is, amongst other things, a development of the English equivalent "why"). The instrumentalist's wind column must perform two functions simultaneously: playing and singing. It's not easy to get the co-ordination of the two elements exactly right and the sense and efficacy of the piece depends on scrupulously respecting the intervals between voice and instrument. Only in this way is it possible to attain the required level of transformation (the vocalization of the instrument and instrumentalization of the voice), and to provide material suitable for further simultaneous levels of transformation: timbre modulations with the mute and modulations of amplitude through "beating" between voice and instrument. In *Sequenza V* there is constant reference to a more simple and elementary level of discourse as contrasted with various other more complex levels. The two simplest stages are interconnected: *unisons* between voice and instrument (and thus the greatest possible degree of acoustic affinity between the two sources of sound) and *periodic articulations* that are initially produced as "beating", when voice and instrument imperceptibly diverge from the unison, and are then propagated through other aspects of the vocal and instrumental execution. Because of the simultaneously grotesque and desperate character of the vocal and instrumental execution and, I suppose, because of its novel aspects, *Sequenza V* has been excessively imitated and plagiarised by the "avant garde".

Certain aspects of *Sequenza III* are related to my previous experiences with *Thema (Omaggio a Joyce)*, which grew out of researches with Eco into poetic onomatopeia, *Circles* and, to a lesser extent, *Visage*. All of these pieces are linked to Cathy Berberian's voice, which was almost a second "*studio di fonologia*" for me. In fact, *Sequenza III* is not only written for Cathy but is about Cathy. I have always been very sensitive, perhaps overly so, to the excess of connotations that the voice carries, whatever it is doing. From the grossest of noises to the most delicate of singing, the voice always means something, always refers beyond itself and creates a huge range of associations: cultural, musical, emotive, physiological, or drawn from everyday life, etc. "Classical" vocal music, whose implicit model was instrumental music, obviously transcended the bitumen of everyday vocal behaviour. As has already been said many times, the voice of a great "classical" singer is a bit like a signed instrument which, as soon as you have finished playing, you put away in a case. It has nothing to do with the voice that the great singer uses to communicate in everyday life. The music of this century has tried to assimilate and control not only every aspect of "classical" singing, but also those aspects which, both because of acoustic considerations and because they disturbed the message, had necessarily been excluded from tonal music – along with the behaviour and the sounds of everyday life.

Sequenza III was very important for me because in it I tried to assimilate many aspects of everyday vocal life, including trivial things like coughing, without losing intermediate levels – laughter becoming coloratura virtuosity for instance – or indeed normal singing. In order to control such a large range of vocal behaviour, I felt I had to break up the text in an apparently devastating way, so as to be able to recuperate fragments from it on different expressive plains, and to reshape them into units that were not discursive but musical. So the text had to be homogeneous, and to lend itself throughout to a project that consisted essentially of confronting and exorcising the excessive connotations, deliberately driven to their furthest limits, on which I had decided, and composing them into musical units. The "modular" text that Mark Kutter wrote for me, consisting of little permutable phrases, was particularly suitable for this operation. It was sufficiently ambiguous to allow for considerable syntactic, and therefore semantic mobility; but at the same time it used an elementary vocabulary with, if you like, an emblematic character to it: I had in fact asked Kutter for a text made up of "universal" words, that could be easily understood and would lodge themselves in the memory (house, night, woman, words, sing etc.) In other words I wanted "*parole sceniche*", bearing in mind, though, that the "theatre" was made up of a restricted and not unduly ambiguous field of phonetic and semantic associations – the sort of thing that your non-specialized listener would be able to grasp and elaborate upon. Basically, the "theatre" is that listener's head: a miniature version, if you like, of what goes on in the landlord's head in *Finnegans Wake*.

D: What did you actually do to Kutter's text?

B: I sifted through Kutter's text using different criteria of segmentation. The first, and most general, distinguishes words, fragments of words, syllables and phonemes (consonants and vowels). But although, when presented in that order, these four elements suggest a progressive loss of meaning, each of them is treated elastically, and from time to time takes over. The words tend to group themselves in series of two, three, or five: the largest significant unit always being a phrase of Kutter's text that is made up in this way. Whereas a succession of word-fragments will never be set out so as to form significant phrases. A succession of syllables won't produce words and, finally, the multiplication of phonetic elements will never lead to the constitution of syllables or other more complex elements. So the text, segmented into its smallest elements (phonemes), its largest elements (five-word phrases), and the various stages in between   all combined in a very mobile fashion – rotates continuously about itself: it is its own text and context. The text will never appear (or be perceived) in its complete form; but all its elements survive the "devastation", and they're all present and take part in different ways. To these criteria for segmenting the text, which produce a continuous passage between maximum and minimum levels of recognizability, I added others that more directly concern the virtuosity of the interpreter. For example, there is an almost regular alternation between the ''spoken'' (everyday gestures of speech) and the ''sung'' (including various ways of singing). But within each class there are so many specified nuances (and also a certain number of timbre modulations and of sounds from outside the vocal tract) that there's never a real opposition between speaking and singing, but rather an extension and transformation of one into the other. When performance tempi are respected, you even get an impression of simultaneous speech and song. In fact, the most obviously (and functionally) virtuoso element in *Sequenza III* is the extreme mobility of vocal characteristics, and the speed of transition from one to another: so much so that there have been a number of sad occasions when Cathy was not performing, on which I have been tempted to transcribe this work for two or three voices. A further criterion of segmentation is provided by the expressive indications that accompany, and dramaturgically condition, the performance. There are about forty emotive suggestions (tense, serene, frantic, coy, desperate, joyful, etc.) which pivot about various forms of laughter – and these, with their speed and regularity of articulation, link up with various vocal characteristics of the previous segmentation. These suggestions of emotional stages succeed each other very rapidly, though they frequently return, and they reinforce in an allusive rather than a concrete fashion the gestural character of each instant. Thus *Sequenza III* is a sort of ''three-part invention'' (segmented text, vocal gesture and ''expression'') – the simultaneous and parallel development of three different aspects that are partially alien to one another, but that interfere, intermodulate and combine into a unity. In other words, it seems to me that in *Sequenza III* the excess of connotations always finds a way forward, a form, whereas the rather elementary semantic ambit of the original text gets disproportionately dilated, rather as if the musical elaboration had acted as a detonator, exploding the text in many different directions. The germ of *Sequenza III* was already

Berio at Oneglia, 1946.

Cathy Berberian with Luigi
Dallapiccola, New York, 1952.

3 Henri Pousseur with Berio at the
RAI, Milan, 1958.

Di lavoro: costituito da una serie di 13 suoni costituita da 2 Territori (A e B) aventi un suono una forma comune (la b) — B è 'l'ultima-costruttivo di A.

B

A

$\uparrow$: . b . b . → ≠ #. q . #.

≠ : . b . j . . b . b . b . → ≠ #. q . q .

Invito la serie contiene ed enunciare in se stessa le 4 forme fondamentali. Per può inoltre separarsi in un senso 'e rapporto di 3 impl. e 3ª Magg = infatti può essere considerato . do punto di vista. traz una sequenza, permetta in tempo e ogni intervallo- 3ª. magg e 3ª minr. La presenza del punto di la b, che stabilisce un rapporto di 'giusta col suono precedente e quello seguente, permette allo sequenza un carattere "aperto".

$\uparrow$ | b . j . . b . b . b . → ≠ | #. q . q . |

$\uparrow$ | 4 q b . (4 q b .) | b . b . → | #. q . |

cioè :
                    3ª
        ⊙——→ b .   b . ——→ #. q . #.
    3ª   3ª

Per la forma contiene più di far A le principio di fraseariazione — Escendari: 1) suoni v'è uniformente un raddoppio (24 q) impl. Da tale raddoppio ossono le cellule di ulteri ... ad esso nella composizione (vedi ... intervallo d'ottava t. battuta 148 e pagg.)

...

4 Excerpts from Berio's analytical notes on *Nones* (1954) illustrating a) relationships within the work's thirteen-note pitch series and b) the numerical values assigned to the elements selected within each parameter: when combined to form a single note, these must add up to nine or more.

Bruno Maderna's lecture notes for the Darmstadt Summer School, 1954, analyzing the opening bars of *Nones* in which four versions of the series (see 4a) are combined

Berio with Pierre Boulez at Baden-Baden, 1960.

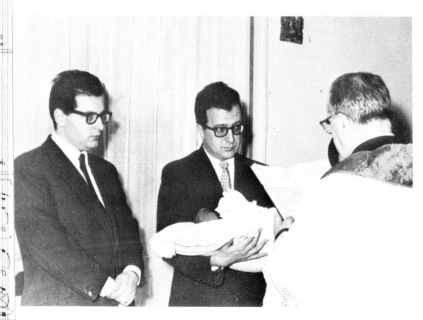

Umberto Eco and Berio at the christening in Milan, 1963, of Eco's son
Stefano – to whom Berio subsequently dedicated *Sincronie*.

0 Berio and Cathy Berberian perform *Folk Songs*, c.1970.

11 Bruno Maderna consults Berio while rehearsing *Differences* for Hilversum radio, 1970.

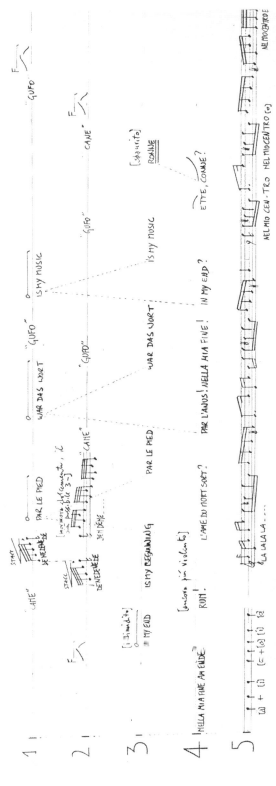

12 A page from the original, five-part version of *A-Ronne* (1974).

a) Edoardo Sanguineti and b) Berio listen to the recording of *A-Ronne* at Hilversum radio, 1974. With Berio is Frans van Rossum, who commissioned the work for the radio station.

there in *Thema (Omaggio a Joyce)*, while *Sequenza III* contains the germ of a more recent work: *A-Ronne*, based on a text by Sanguineti.

D: Apart from lacking a text, do the other Sequenzas *have anything in common?*

B: All the other *Sequenzas* for solo instruments are intended to set out and melodically develop an essentially harmonic discourse and to suggest, particularly in the case of the monodic instruments, a polyphonic mode of listening. When I started the series, back in 1958, I wasn't using the term "polyphonic" in any metaphorical sense, as I would now when working with monodic instruments, but literally. I wanted to establish a way of listening so strongly conditioned as to constantly suggest a latent, implicit counterpoint. The ideal was the "polyphonic" melodies of Bach. An inaccessible ideal, naturally, because what implicitly guided polyphonic listening in a Bach melody was nothing less than the history of baroque musical language, whereas in a "non-linguistic" melody like my *Sequenza* for flute, history provided no protection, and everything had to be planned out explicitly. But although it was a bit utopian, the experience was extremely useful to me. As often happens in scientific research when, in pursuit of what appears to be the principal objective, so many interesting side-issues emerge that the direction of the research becomes modified, so, in pursuing my ideal of implicit polyphony, I discovered melody's heterophonic possibilities. The title was meant to underline that the piece was built from a sequence of harmonic fields (as indeed are almost all the *Sequenzas)* from which the other, strongly characterized musical functions were derived. It's the principle of *more* or *less* that governs the flute *Sequenza*, if I can put it that way. It's used not to produce ambiguous, "open" and interchangeable structures, but to control the density of the melody as it proceeds. I mean by that a qualitative control of density and not merely – or not necessarily – a control of the quantity of events at any given moment.

The temporal, dynamic, pitch and morphological dimensions

of the piece are characterized by maximum, medium and minimum levels of tension. The level of maximum tension (which is also an *exceptional* one relative to the norm of conventional playing) within the temporal dimension is produced by moments of maximum speed in articulation and moments of maximum duration of sounds, the medium level is always established by a neutral distribution of fairly long notes and fairly rapid articulations, and the minimum level entails silence, or a tendency to silence. The pitch dimension is at its maximum level when notes jump about within a wide gamut and establish the tensest intervals, or when they insist on extreme registers: the medium and minimum levels follow logically from this. The maximum level of the dynamic dimension is naturally produced by moments of maximum sound energy and maximum dynamic contrast. What I call the morphological dimension is placed, in certain of its aspects, at the service of the other three and is, as it were, their rhetorical instrument. It seeks to define degrees of acoustic transformation relative to an inherited model which in this case is the flute with all its historical and acoustic connotations. Thus a level of maximum tension within the morphological dimension is obtained when the image, *my* image of the flute, is drastically altered with flutter tongues, key clicks and double stops (two notes at once). I contented myself with very little when you think about it, granted that at the time you couldn't really change the image of the flute without at least playing it underwater. But the flutter tongues are almost always used as the furthest extension of rapid articulation, the key clicks as the furthest extension of a progressive move towards noise realized by using the lowest register, maximum speed, maximum intervallic tension and flutter tongue: so the key clicks round off a process that is already underway. As for the double stops (those famous *g-c*s and *a-d*s that started off the hubbub of multiphonics, which seems finally to be quietening down), their function is more symbolic than actual: to some extent they stand for my desperate search for polyphony with the most monodic instrument in history. Finally, the extreme density of the melodic writing is ensured by the fact that at any one time *at least* two of the four dimensions that I've described are at the maximum level of tension. In fact, here too, as in *Sequenza III* for voice, if the tempo relationships are accurately respected, you sometimes get the impression if not of polyphony, at least of simultaneous events. The piece is very difficult, and I therefore adopted a notation that was very precise, but allowed a margin of flexibility in order that the player might have the freedom – psychological rather than musical – to adapt the piece here and there to his technical stature. But instead, this notation has allowed many players – none of them by any means shining examples of professional integrity – to perpetrate adaptations that were little short of piratical. In fact, I hope to rewrite *Sequenza I* in rhythmic notation: maybe it will be less "open" and more authoritarian, but at least it will be reliable.

Control of the development of harmony and melodic density is a feature common to all the *Sequenzas*, though it takes different forms because, in each case, certain aspects of the instrument's technique are examined critically. Take *Sequenza II* for harp, for example. French "impressionism" has left us with a rather limited vision of this instrument: as if its most characteristic feature were that it could only be played by half-naked girls with long, blond hair, who confine themselves to drawing seductive glissandi from it. But the harp has another, harder, stronger and more determined side to it, one which the modern school of Salzedo has helped to establish. *Sequenza II* aims to focus on some of these characteristics, and to make them appear simultaneously: at certain moments it must sound like a forest with the wind blowing through it.

D: Are you ever stimulated by games – the game of being able to do something with a given material that, to a greater or lesser extent, is resistant to manipulation?

B: I wouldn't know. I don't really understand what games have to do with it, but maybe they do happen, and if they do, it means that everything was predetermined by things that have absolutely nothing to do with the game itself. I've always felt the need to cover a rather wide field of action, research and musical expression, so it's likely, indeed certain, that once in a while I decide to amuse myself. But it's equally true that within this rather wide area I tend to move quickly, and I'll leave the game as quickly as I started it, to retreat to my lair. In fact it's no accident that often I instinctively find myself working on different projects at the same time, amusing myself with one and sweating blood over another. But it's the tendency towards reunion that justifies the tendency to many-sidedness. This is not the time for cutting diamonds: there's thunder in the air and one must do everything quickly and well. And there's no point in complaining, as did Joyce in an early essay that he wrote for the University of Padua that even the "journalist" has found a place in the monk's chair.

Another thing I don't understand is this business of material resisting play and manipulation. For me, musical material means thought, muscial concepts, and I hardly think it possible that it should resist itself any more than a word might resist its meaning. It's the physical aspect, as I was saying earlier when talking about virtuosity, that can sometimes offer a certain resistance to conceptual material, and it is precisely this resistance (though it's never enough by itself) that provokes the search for new relations between the conceptual and physical, and even the "discovery" of new physical resources: steel in architecture and the frame of the modern piano, plastic in sculpture, oscillators in electronic music . . .

D: When I was talking about your relationship to the material I meant something else. I was thinking of the many composers who, through terror of subjective content, declare themselves to be quite detached from the compositional process and limit themselves to observing the material forming itself according to more or less fortuitous processes.

B: Yes, I've heard about such things, and it seems to me that the attitude involved represents a sort of "great refusal" only slightly more advanced than the pianist in evening dress walking around the piano without playing it. I assume this is what you are talking about. Once, automatic serial procedures (those of Boulez's *Structures I* or Maderna's *Quartetto*) were "programmed" to produce constantly differing combinations of the same series of pitches, durations, etc. Chance didn't enter into it, not so much because chance in music doesn't exist, but simply because these were rather elementary means for producing and controlling musical situations that tended towards the statistical but were rigorously circumscribed. On that basis you can invent an infinite number of automatic procedures (though it would be better not to waste your time: the computer can prepare you several hundred thousand in a few seconds), and you can "programme" them not to proliferate abstract serial proportions, but to transform and proliferate anything you like, even two bars from "Casta Diva". At a first "reading", for example, every time the tonic, f, appears in the bass clef it becomes g_b, and every time it appears in the treble clef it becomes b, while all the as and cs become a_b and d_b at regular intervals. The overall duration of the fragment remains the same, but within it proportions change here and there, as do registers. The overall duration of the fragment is then reduced in a discontinuous fashion while the internal proportions tend to expand so that the original material can no longer be entirely contained within it; however, the bits left over will be used later when . . . etc. etc. The procedure begins to interest me when the duration of the fragment and its internal proportions have been so reduced that there's practically nothing left. It reminds me of those terrible machines at car dumps that grab an old car and crush it until it's no bigger than a suitcase: I've only seen them in films, and usually there's a dead body inside. By all means pulverize Bellini (frankly, I reckon he deserves it), but I'd be a bit more careful with the others . . . The fact is that these procedures have their roots not in chance but in paranoia, and in evading so-called subjective choices (though if you push them out of the door, they'll come back in through the window) – the paranoia of someone who's afraid, and wants to create an illusion of order. And in hypocrisy: just think of how many choices you'd have to make in order to make the wretched procedure instrumentally attractive. People who make themselves a poetics out of proliferating other people's material with semi-automatic procedures make me feel slightly sick. It needs the irony, the speculative and slightly talmudic brain of Kagel to give a sense to the systematic exploitation of other people's musical (and not only musical) work. It needs the genius of Sanguineti to give an ethical, as well as a poetic sense to the mass of allusions, the universal work that inhabits his poetry.

D: So you think it's technically impossible for material to "produce itself"?

B: Absolutely impossible. It always needs petrol that you've paid through the nose for, and an engine to transform it into energy.

D: In your previous answers you've touched on some of the more delicate aspects of composition: the relationship between composer and performer, the dialectic between the subjectivity of the 'I' that manipulates and the objectivity of the material that is manipulated. In this perspective, where you resolve the will/chance opposition in favour of the former, how do you view the relationship between compositional technique and the will to express? In other words, what direction, what orientation, do you give to your manipulatory capacities?

B: It's not really a matter of manipulatory capacities (I find that a somewhat degrading expression), but of the ability to transform. We're always dealing with models, even those that we make for ourselves, and our work consists in widening the field of transformational paths until we manage to transform one thing into another, as in a fairy tale. Shall I tell you what my theatrical ideal is? Well, it's to take two simple and banal forms of behaviour, say "walking in the rain" and "typing" and to put them on stage in such a way that they transform one another and produce by morphogenesis a third form of behaviour: we don't really know what this is because we've never seen it before, and it's not the elementary combination of the two familiar forms of behaviour. If this is to happen, either in theatre or music, the forms of behaviour must be recognizable. In classical forms, for example, the "recognizable behaviour" was a theme, one motif, then another, and perhaps another after that. They may well come loaded with structural functions and generative properties, but they've also got eyes, nose and a mouth that make them attractive and recognizable amidst the crowd of other presences that they themselves have given rise to. So they become for us signals of deeper events, and when they reappear, heavy with their many functions and different meanings, we feel grateful for it. It's this continuous sense of gratitude that makes Massimo Mila's book on Beethoven *Lettura della Nona Sinfonia* so attractive. Not that I give more importance to beautiful melodies and unforgettable themes than to the structural functions and intellectual organization of classical and romantic musical discourse. On the contrary. But if the deeper structure is to influence what we hear *structurally,* then there must be many links, a hierarchy of many different signals that can at least potentially be deciphered and recognized – even though sometimes these signals are destined to disappear, to be swept away and absorbed by the events that they have themselves initiated, as often happens to Beethoven's themes. But the virtual recognizability of these signals, these thematic faces with their expressive peculiarities, is of fundamental importance. One of the reasons for the objective difficulties involved in coming to grips with the neo-classical Schoenberg of, say, the *Wind Quintet* is – quite apart from the general incompatibility and indifference between rhythm and harmony – the frankly repulsive character of the dodeca-phonic "themes" which disfigure the discourse, and whose useless recurrence I find utterly depressing. The same sort of depression that comes over me for other reasons when I start reading Schenker's harmonic analyses. His appeals to Ideals and Nature do little to conceal the squalor and structural irrelevance of his analyses, as if music (which as far as he's concerned stops with Brahms) was only made up of "grammatical" chords devoid of any real temporal dimension, any thematic physiognomy, and any contrapuntal substance. Of course, classical form with its tonal and harmonic structures and all the other things that have contributed to making it the supreme and universal architecture of musical sense is a projection of mind – not merely of history and musical experience – but to reduce all this to a strategy, a manipulation of degrees of the scale, is a very long shot indeed. It's a pity that by the time Schenker was writing, the old-time Viennese pranksters had disappeared: one of them could have played a rather dirty, but significant trick on him, because he certainly didn't have perfect pitch, or he'd have dissected his corpses in a different way. They could have played him a Beethoven symphony, but used a sneaky modulation so as to arrive at the recapitulation a semi-tone up, and thus show him that, in spite of the arbitrary operation, the symphony came out of it almost unharmed, precisely because of what he ignores. Schenker's theories about first, second and third levels of harmonic articulation have a sinister ring and remind me of a concentration camp with three barbed wire fences round it. And nothing in the middle except death. But we've got rather a long way away from your question. Or perhaps not. Basically, everything can be transformed, not just melodies and memorable physiognomies, but even the idea of transformation itself. But there is one problem: even though transformational procedures always signify something, this doesn't guarantee them an expressive meaning.

D: One particularly striking aspect of your music is your taste for reclaiming, or at any rate using, musical materials belonging to other spheres, such as jazz, folklore – even pop songs.

B: I wouldn't have thought it was a very striking aspect, though certainly I have concerned myself with all of them. But not through any taste for reclaiming things. Every contact with these "other spheres" has had different motivations. For example, there's a brief jazz episode in *Laborintus II* at the end of Sanguineti's "harangue" against usury, with interruptions from Dante and Pound. Amongst other things, *Laborintus II* is a "tracking shot" showing the many different ways in which an instrumental group (whose composition is very like a jazz orchestra) and a vocal group, or an instrumental group and electronic music, can be integrated. So the reference to jazz is one amongst many: perhaps it's the most obvious because its ingredients are, deliberately, the most banal thing to appear in the (entirely invented) musical catalogue that is *Laborintus II*. Moreover, Sanguineti's text is conceived somewhat in the spirit of the mediaeval catalogue: like the music, it too is a tracking shot that moves slowly, but with salutary jumps (real changes of poetic scene) from Isidore of Seville's *Etymologies* through to Sanguineti himself. So the inventory of *Laborintus II*'s musical catalogue would be a wide-ranging one, and I wouldn't know where to begin describing it; there's a jazz episode, true enough, the voices are all amplified, and there's no reference to traditional "cultivated" singing . . . I'm rather pleased with the sound of *Laborintus II*, with the coherence and acoustic homogeneity of the ensemble, in spite of the disparate techniques and means that are used in it. It compensates for the relative formal simplicity of the piece, which proceeds by contrasting, but often recurrent and circular episodes: I avoided large-scale developments. Basically, *Laborintus II* is a didactic piece (it presents no excessive technical difficulites): in fact, when I've had the chance to prepare and conduct it in certain American universities – where there is no problem in finding all the necessary performers – it seemed easier to me to realize the true spirit of the work than in the formal, concert-hall situation.

As for pop songs, well, I must confess that I wrote two for Cathy Berberian on texts by Calvino; they're a part of the mime-ballet *Allez-Hop*, but they have no real musical function: they're part of the scenery, like a cupboard or a tree or a fountain. You could even put something else in their place.

D: You also used popular songs in Passaggio, *but you didn't specify which ones.*

B: It's a gesture for which I could have given rather more precise directions. It happens when the two "enemy" choruses, one in the orchestra, and one distributed among the audience, meet momentarily on the same word ("*libera*"), from which they take off in full cry, and in different directions: the chorus in the audience singing musical fetishes (which can be substituted at will), while the other one sings songs with political connotations, linked to the struggle for liberation. The result is a vocal magma that is only just differentiated by the vocal behaviour of the two groups, and their different placing within the theatre, but a magma that is immediately redeemed by the instruments, and the "victorious" singing of the chorus in the orchestra. It is one of many passages from distinct to indistinct, from . . . to . . ., of which the score of *Passaggio* essentially consists.

My relationship with folk music is of a different kind: it's not anecdotal as my relationships with jazz and pop music have been. My interest in folklore is of very long standing – even as a boy I was writing pastiche folksongs. Recently this interest has put down deeper roots, and I've tried to gain a more specific and technical understanding of the processes that govern certain folk idioms, to which I've been particularly attracted because, putting it simply and egoistically, they can teach me something useful. I'm thinking particularly of Sicilian and Serbo-croat folk music and the "heterophonies" of central Africa. I'm not an ethnomusic-ologist, just a pragmatic egoist: so I tend to be interested only in those folk techniques and means of expression that I can in one way or other assimilate without a stylistic break, and that allow me to take a few steps forward in the search for a unity underlying musical worlds that are apparently alien to one another.

D: To go back to the principle of transformation that you were talking about before. How do you connect your use of folklore, whether as gesture or as process, with the function that quotation and self-quotation have in your work? I'm thinking of a work like Sinfonia, *for instance.*

B: There's a very close link, provided that you don't view the third part of *Sinfonia*, to which you're no doubt referring, as a *collage* of quotes. I'm not interested in *collages*, and they amuse me only when I'm doing them with my children; then they become an exercise in relativizing and "decontextualizing" images, an elementary exercise whose healthy cynicism won't do anyone any harm. This third part of *Sinfonia* has a skeleton which is the scherzo from Mahler's *Second Symphony* – a skeleton that often re-emerges fully fleshed out, then disappears, then comes back again . . . But it's never alone: it's accompanied throughout by the "history of music" that it itself recalls for me, with all its many levels and references – or at least those bits of history that I was able to keep a grip on, granted that often there's anything up to four different references going on at the same time. So the scherzo of Mahler's *Second Symphony* becomes a generator of harmonic functions and of musical references that are pertinent to them which appear, disappear, pursue their own courses, return to Mahler, cross paths, transform themselves into Mahler or hide behind it. The references to Bach, Brahms, Boulez, Berlioz, Schoenberg, Stravinsky, Strauss, Stockhausen etc. are therefore *also* signals which indicate which harmonic country we are going through, like bookmarkers, or little flags in different colours stuck into a map to indicate salient points during an expedition full of surprises.

I'd had it in mind for a long time to explore from the inside a piece of music from the past: a creative exploration that was at the same time an analysis, a commentary and an extension of the original. This follows from my principle that, for a composer, the best way to analyze and comment on a piece is to do something, using materials from that piece. The most profitable commentary on a symphony or an opera has always been another symphony or another opera. My *Chemins* are the best analyses of my *Sequenzas*, just as the third part of my *Sinfonia* is the most developed commentary that I could have possibly produced on a piece by Mahler. But originally, the idea of this third part of *Sinfonia* was linked not to Mahler, but to Beethoven. I was in fact thinking of harmonically "exploding" the last three movements of Beethoven's *Quartet in C sharp minor*, Op. 131 – though without quotations, and with "little flags" composed by me instead. The vocal parts would have had a more instrumental character and the text would naturally have been quite different. I finally opted for Mahler not only because his music proliferates spontaneously, but also because it allowed me to extend, transform and comment on all of its aspects: including that of orchestration. I needed, that is, a structural basis that could be recognized every so often in its original form. Translating Beethoven's Op.131 into orchestral terms would have been a very risky operation and, in view of the task in hand, not an entirely justified one. And using Mahler was also a tribute to Leonard Bernstein who has doen so much for his music. As you know, *Sinfonia* is dedicated to him.

However, this voyage to Cithera on board a Mahlerian vessel only acquires a complete sense when it is itself the subject of commentary in the fifth and final part of *Sinfonia*, which is by far the most complex because it takes up, transforms and comments on all the others. The first four parts of *Sinfonia* are to the fifth as Mahler's scherzo is to the third. Thus the skeleton, the carrying structure of the fifth part, is made up of the four preceding parts, though they often appear in summary fashion – sometimes almost like shorthand, but at other times complete. But the order in which the fragments appear is changed. For example, the second part appears complete, transcribed from one end to the other, alongside salient elements from the third part and some from the first – and also some new elements that have been forming in the meantime. Thus the second part becomes the carrying structure for many other previously heard elements which appear as contracted fragments, assimilated instrumentally and vocally with new elements that comment on the commentary . . . The unforeseen and discontinuous dislocation of previously heard events provokes a sort of block in the (musical) stream of consciousness that characterized the previous parts, and par-ticularly the third. The memory is continually stimulated and put to work, only to be contradicted and frustrated. It's finally onto an element from the first part that the whole development converges, thus becoming more homogeneous and unanimous. The first part never came to a proper ending, it suddenly stopped and remained open. The fifth part concludes *Sinfonia* by bringing to an end the suspended development of the first. Thus the third part of *Sinfonia* is both the centre and the macroscopic model of the entire work. It also has a centrifugal function in as much as its mechanisms involve the totality of the work, projecting and amassing fragments of that totality in the fifth part.

As you can see, we're a long way away from a *collage* of quotations. *Sinfonia* is a very homogeneous work that looks within itself. The text is treated in a way that is analogous to the musical development, and is very complex. David Osmond-Smith has finished a long and exhaustive study of *Sinfonia* that pays particular attention to the way the texts are used. Simplifying as much as possible, what happens is that the first part of *Sinfonia* elaborates fragments from a text by Claude Lévi-Strauss *(Le cru et le cuit)*, as if they were starting points for a narration that is continually interrupted. It's Lévi-Strauss as a great writer that we're dealing with here and not, in any explicit way, Lévi-Strauss as a great anthropologist. As I was saying earlier, this first part also has an interrupted musical development – just as it looks as though it's turning into a concerto for piano and orchestra; it's a development which will be taken up again and seen through to an end in the fifth and last part. The second part has a totally different musical structure, and it has no text as such, only an alternation of phonetic elements that lead to the gradual "disclosure" and enunciation of the name of the black martyr Martin Luther King. Or rather "O Martin Luther King" – so as to give greater continuity and completeness to the sequence of vowels. The third part has a pilot text by Samuel Beckett (taken from *The Unnamable)*, a proliferating text that provides a parallel to Mahler's proliferating musical "text". One of the most important proliferations of the Beckett text (though not the only one) is the sequence of verbal signs which describe, sometimes metaphorically, sometimes explicitly, the various stages of the harmonic voyage, musically marked and punctuated by the quotations. The fourth part remains fixated on the first two notes and the first two words of the fourth movement of Mahler's *Second Symphony* – the latter translated into French so as to allow a fleeting link with an image of Lévi-Strauss's *"appel bruyant"*. Thus "O Röschen roth *(rose de sang appel bruyant)"*. Finally, the fifth part parallels the music by taking up fragments from the texts of the four previous parts. The interrupted fragments of Lévi-Strauss as great writer that appeared in the first part are finally completed, the discourse is conducted to one of its possible conclusions, and as in the structure of the music, the use of the text suggests that it may have not only a poetic, but also a scientific basis. In fact, it's only then that I try to pay homage to Lévi-Strauss as a great anthropologist.

A new recording of *Sinfonia* conducted by Pierre Boulez with the Orchestre Nationale de Paris is about to come out. The existing one is unfortunately incomplete because, as so often happens, it was recorded immediately after the first performance of the first four parts in New York in 1968. I managed to finish the fifth part only three months later, when I had thoroughly convinced myself of its necessity.

D: Does quotation always have this function in your works?

B: Apart from the *Chemins,* where I quote, translate, expand and transcribe my *Sequenzas,* I don't recall having quoted anything else, if you can define my use of the Mahler as quotation in any case. I've certainly made allusions here and there, but no more than Wagner did when he revived King Mark from *Tristan* in *Die Meistersinger,* or D'Annunzio recalling a famous verse from the first Canto of the *Purgatorio* in *I Pastori,* or Beethoven quoting Mozart's *Don Giovanni* in the *Diabelli Variations,* or Alban Berg quoting *Tristan* in the *Lyric Suite.*

D: Sinfonia, Sequenza III *and* Folk Songs *are among your best known and best loved pieces; even children at elementary school like* Sequenza III! *But are there not one or two of your pieces that have met with resistance, if not outright rejection from the public? I'm thinking, for instance, of a performance of* Allez-Hop *which took place at the end of the Sixties and aroused some very lively negative reactions.*

B: It's natural that children should like *Sequenza III;* they like *Visage* too. After all, both pieces have links with a reality that they already know, albeit not a strictly musical one. But I can assure you that these two pieces were not intended for children, on the contrary . . . As for *Allez-Hop*, I think that ten or fifteen years ago in Bologna or Rome one took the reactions of the public more or less for granted: a preconceived and programmatic rejection of contemporary music was customary. Musicially, *Allez-Hop* presents no problems. And the relationship between music and action on stage is very clear. But in all the productions of it – some of which have been of considerable quality – there has always been a tendency to complicate the action, and to exaggerate and overload the situations, whereas the music demands a direct and immediate theatre, made up of intense gestures rather in the Brechtian manner, that are without redundancy and have a certain purity of image. It's a fairly brief piece (about half an hour), and it ought to just slide past like a film; instead, producers have all too often inserted pauses between one section and the next in order to develop their pantomimes and have complicated things excessively. The production for those long-gone perform-ances in Rome and Bologna was by Mario Missiroli, and was rather beautiful. But I must admit that at Rome, where I was conducting, there was a certain ill-will on our part towards the public and Roman officialdom. We wanted to finish off *Allez-Hop* with a lightly ironic touch but, as so often happens, it transformed itself into something that was no longer quite so light-hearted . . . At the last minute I had added a final piece for orchestra, with electric guitars, drum-kit etc. during which the mimes came down from the stage and, adopting the attitudes of the then current "flower generation", circulated around the stalls painting the heads of distinguished elderly gentlemen and the *décolletés* of the more showy matrons. All hell broke loose, of course. Our malevolence was in part based on the fact that at the time there was a fairly explicit link between the neo-fascists and the prosperous, right-wing bourgeoisie who frequented the Opera. But a week before the first night a dreadful thing had happened to me and Mario. We were attacked by a gang of fascists who were going past the Opera singing "*per vincere ci vogliono i leoni di Mussolini*" ("to win you need the lions of Mussolini"). I suppose we asked for it, because we were making fun of them like a couple of students. Mario came out of it with a broken finger, and I with a cracked vertebra. The police watched imperturbably, with arms folded, as the "massacre" went on. This episode certainly helped to translate our originally ironic intentions into an angry gesture. . . .

D: Earlier, when you were talking about your Chemins, *you mentioned transcription. What do you mean by transcription?*

B: The history of transcription has yet to be written, and if I were still teaching, that is something that I'd like to go into with my students. I'd start with Monteverdi's *Orfeo* ("This ritornello was played by two ordinary violins . . .") and then pause over Bach transcribing Bach. I'd take a quick look at Liszt: his transcriptions and paraphrases, which combine cosmopolitan high fashion with a concern for popularization, made an enormous contribution to the evolution of piano technique and to the exchanging of musical influences, but they have little to do with his great personality as a composer. I'd take an equally quick look at Busoni: his great personality as a transcriber has little to do with his rather frustrating work as a composer. Thus I'm interested in transcription when it's part of a design, a coherent and homogeneous musical vision, even though at times it's primarily motivated by considerations of practicality and custom. Then I'd look at Schoenberg transcribing himself and Brahms, Ravel transcribing himself, and Stravinsky transcribing "everything". I'd also look at isolated but very significant episodes such as Maderna transcribing Gabrieli, Ghedini transcribing Frescobaldi and Kagel who also transcribes literally everything. But the real object of this course would be to arrive at unconscious transcription, in other words, forms of transcription that are completely assimilated into the creative process. Here we are no longer dealing with transcription as a genre (don't forget that for centuries the practice of transcription had a function analogous to that of records), but as part of the ups and downs of creativity: when, that is, you have a single musical vision (a single project, they say these days) going through different and self sufficient formulations before arriving at the definitive realization, decanted from (or destroying) all the others. There are three works that particularly interest me in this respect: *Noces* (there are three versions of this Stravinskian masterpiece), Stockhausen's *Kontrapunkte* (the first, unperformable version was for a huge orchestra: I have the impression that Stockhausen was "born" precisely by reducing, that is, transcribing this work for ten instruments), and Boulez's *Notations* (a large work for orchestra that transcribes and amplifies some short pieces for piano written in 1947). Naturally, I would contribute to the project with my *Chemins,* and also my *Concerto* for two pianos and orchestra where, from time to time, the two solo instruments coexist with their image reflected and transcribed in the orchestra.

D: Your works give a predominant role to the voice, and therefore to a verbal text, normally poetry. Is setting a text to music rather like transcribing it for you? What relationship do you have with the semantic element in language, treating it as a musician?

B: Yes, it's a form of transcription, and I normally have an excellent relationship with the semantic aspect of a text because I have a great respect for it and treat it with all the musical honours of which I am capable. Heidegger said that language "is the house of life" and, as everyone knows, it is also a marvellous, untiring machine for the production of meaning. Music is a further machine that amplifies and transcribes that meaning onto a different level of perception and intelligence – provided that it respects all the aspects of language, including the acoustic one.

D: Some composers say that recourse to language is a way of giving greater semantic density to music, whereas you turn the tables, asserting that music allows one to further augment the semantic capacities of language.

B: The point of view that you mention may be justified from the point of view of historical development, but it's not intrinsic to the relationship between words and music. Perhaps what they mean is that at certain crucial moments in the evolution of music, musicians will venture into unexplored territory with more confidence when there is, in any case, one significant dimension to support them – that, precisely, of language. But in the majority of cases, in the most musically significant situations (Schoenberg's *Pierrot lunaire* and Stockhausen's *Gesang der Jünglinge*, for example), word and voice are the protagonists of these steps into the unknown, and it is thanks to them, and not thanks to their amiable protection, that new musical territories are discovered.

I'm interested in music that mimes and, in a certain sense, describes that prodigious phenomenon that lies at the heart of language: sound becoming sense. Because of this it's important to also have an acoustic understanding of the verbal material, so as to be able to re-enter and reconquer sense through the acoustic dimension. Perhaps it's because of this that I greatly dislike syllabic vocal music, with one syllable for every note, as if the organization (usually "dodecaphonic") of the notes had something in common with the organization of syllables in words and phrases. The only really successfully syllabic vocal music is perhaps that of Debussy: but in this case it's the instruments that *sing* the words, extending, amplifying and completing a vocal line that, instead, almost speaks the words. I think it was Schoenberg who wrote somewhere (it's remained stamped on my memory, but I can't recall where I read it) that syllabic units are primary, natural and therefore raw, while phonetic units provide the dynamic element of language. The units, therefore, of the instinctive improviser on one hand, and those of the composer on the other, as I was saying earlier.

D: *One dimension that you've not mentioned is that of the formal function of poetry; yet at the moment in which form as something that in some way precedes the work dissolves, at the moment in which music, like other artistic systems, questions the principle of causality, and the necessary dependence of consequent on antecedent, certain composers – Webern amongst them – have sought in the poetic text not only conceptual contents, but also a form that constituted a sort of guarantee of continuity and "logical" concreteness for their music.*

B: I don't think you can look at Webern in this way. Anton Webern carries with him the last echo of the romantic Lied; in his work the relation between text and music is inextricable, and I wouldn't like to say which has primacy from the formal point of view. Indeed, I'd rather say the contrary: that his musical processes and procedures are so intense and concentrated, and so strongly spiritually charged, that they impose their own dimension on Hildegard Jone – and that these in turn lend themselves admirably to all the sinuosities and truncations of Webern's music. It was above all with Mozart and Schubert that the pre-established forms of poetic narration coincided with the music in a miraculous fashion, and on all levels including the psychological. Then music and poetry spoke the same language, and all it needed was a minimal disjunction between the two (for example, a melodic variation when repeating the same poetic strophe) to open up abysses of sense: think of Schubert's *Winterreise* or Schumann's *Dichterliebe* and what happens in them to the relation between poetic strophe and musical "strophe". In other words, poetry and music move symmetrically and analogically not only on the rhetorical level, but also on that of *langue* and *parole*. But you'd look in vain for that in Webern. Indeed, Webern's vocal music always emits something indefinable, a sort of expressive stupor that derives from a certain impassivity (I would hardly dare to call it indifference) of the music in the face of the text. Even when the discourse becomes strophic, this impassivity remains, as for example in the final part of the second *Cantata* (where the text is "ground up" by a quadruple cancrizan canon repeated three times) which becomes an icy machine of divine contemplation, an implacable prayer. However, the relationship between text and music in Webern is sufficiently complex and ambiguous to permit all sorts of considerations, some of them very contrasting. I don't believe it's necessarily the text that confers a formal sense on the music, or in any way functions as a formal support for it. It's rather the type of relation or "conflict" with the text and, above all, the type of vocal writing that one chooses – or by which one lets oneself be chosen – that has formal consequences. It's an old story. Generalizing and simplifying a great deal, you could say that before Monteverdi instrumental music was an extension of vocal music. After Monteverdi vocal music became an extension, an *alter ego* of instrumental music. In Mozart the two tendencies, having reached the pitch of maturity, coexist in a miraculous equilibrium, never heard before or since. I could give hundreds of examples; just think of one of greatest: the vocal quality of the *G minor Quintet* K. 516. You have to wait until Stravinsky to find a roughly analogous equilibrium. The fact is that gestures and discourses, verbal as much as musical, come to symbolize in the course of time past cultural and expressive functions – and thus become "archetypal" gestures. We see it in the musical theatre of Mozart and Stravinsky, where music seems to come back to the opera house, bringing with it the gestures and discourses of the concert hall. Just as sometimes music seems to enter the concert hall bringing with it an "operatic" past. I'd say that Stravinsky used technical and expressive archetypes throughout his work – particularly the all-pervasive Russian "vocality".

D: For you, the voice as a "natural" musical instrument has almost acted as a thread running through thirty years of work. But you've maintained an equally constant interest in the most technological of means: electronic resources. How do you explain this apparent contradiction?

B: I'd say that there hasn't been any contradiction because my first important work of electronic music (perhaps I should say electro-acoustic music) derived from the voice: *Thema (Omaggio a Joyce)*. My first contact with the possibilities of these new resources came about, strangely enough, in 1952 at the Museum of Modern Art in New York, during a concert dedicated for the most part to Varèse, and conducted by Leopold Stokowsky. I say "strangely enough" because I was completely in the dark as to what Mayer-Eppler and Eimert were preparing in Germany, and I knew only by word of mouth what Pierre Schaeffer was doing in Paris. Anyway, in that concert in New York there was the first performance of a piece of tape music, based on the elementary manipulation of piano sounds recorded on tape. It was called *Sonic contours,* and the authors were Luening and Ussachewsky: it was an experience devoid of musical content, entirely innocuous, but I was left with a vivid impression of new sounds, and of what could be done with magnetic tape, and cutting up sound with scissors. When I got back to Italy a few weeks later, I immediately began experimenting for myself on the RAI's tape recorders, in the Corso Sempione studios: every request for incidental music became an excuse for electro-acoustic experiment. The support of Dr. Lietti at the RAI and my encounters with Pousseur, Maderna and Stockhausen did the rest. The tape pieces that I realized before 1957 were preparatory work as far as I was concerned. I began to feel at my musical ease with *Perspectives,* a piece in which the extreme acceleration of little sound cells with different characteristics transformed relation-ships of duration and frequency into timbre. It was the experience of *Perspectives* that allowed me, in the months that followed, to realize *Thema (Omaggio a Joyce)* and *Différences.* It even influenced the composition of *Circles,* where there's no electronic music (it's written for female voice, harp and two percussionists, and sets poetry by e.e. cummings), but where the text's acoustic families organize, and are mirrored by all the instrumental character-istics. In effect, the instrumental parts are organized around a continuum of vocal sounds and modes of attack ranging from vowels pure and simple through to the various families of consonants. The rapid, statistically based mingling of "vocal models" produces a sort of supervocalization of the instrumental ensemble that tends to assimilate the voice. In other words, the eternal theme of transformation, which has gone through enor-mous developments as a result of the experiences of electronic music.

I believe that if one day a greater rapport is achieved between the various musical genres, and the various citadels of musical consumption, this will be due in part to the experiences of electronic music. Including those experiences that involve substantially neutral operations, which are indifferent to the instrinsic cultural connotations of the musical material that they seek to transform. Often it's precisely those researches that momentarily preclude "content" which may become part of deep and richly significant levels of experience later on. What has happened, and is currently happening more than ever in electronic music research is in certain respects similar to what has happened in linguistics, where the pursuit of research into a "universal" grammar has of necessity put the genuinely semantic (and indeed expressive) dimensions of language rather into the background. But that's another story . . .

INTERVIEW 6

with Rossana Dalmonte

D: A propos of electronic music, should we these days still be talking about "experiments" or thinking in terms of "works"? Is the composer still at the research stage, or does he by now feel able to use established means to achieve specific results?

B: The real work is always that of looking for potential tendencies, and not for those already operating – and therefore experimenting. However, the boundary between experiment and work is a very artifical and ideological one. Consider Beethoven's *Ninth Symphony:* basically it's an enormous experiment, with results that everybody knows. I simply mean that without an interest in the evolution of ideas and musical means – and therefore without its experimental aspect – music as an expression of ideas would have been dead quite a while back. But the case of electronic music is a very special one. In the Fifties and Sixties, studies in analogue electronic music (where the musician manually and continuously controlled electrical waves that were *analogous* to the wave forms of sound) existed for the purpose of producing musical works. During the Seventies, and even before, studies in electronic music changed technologies, and existed to perfect themselves . . . Thus twenty or thirty years ago the musican shaped technical means of non-musical origin (oscillators, filters, tape-recorders etc.) to his own ideas and visions, whereas during the last ten or fifteen years one gets the impression that technical development has got the upper hand, and that the composer is struck dumb in the face of the new resources created expressly for him. In other words, if in the past – even the distant past – music was often the testing bench and the stimulus for scientific research, and thus music tended to draw scientific knowledge to it, in more recent years you get the impression that it's now science that draws music to it and takes possession of it. Indeed, you often get the impression that a scientific creativity applicable to music has substituted itself for musical creativity, and that musical thought has regressed to the level of the (invariably squalid) opinions that an electronic engineer from Bell Telephone or a Stanford "software man" may have about music. Mind you, I'm only talking about impressions, because in reality things are rather more complex and articulated, and rather more deep-rooted. The experiences gained in electronic music during the '50s were evidently of fundamental importance, but it quickly became apparent how futile and inane was, amongst many others, the notion that loudspeakers had to be used principally to produce "new sounds" in the concert hall – whereas instruments and voices were there to produce "old sounds". It was also realized that "the infinite possibilities of electronic music" was an empty phrase (I don't think I ever said it myself, even amidst the enthusiasm of the roaring Fifties) because those possibilities above all concerned the acoustic and manipulatory levels of music, and not the conceptual one, which dwindled rapidly away to make room for a clutter of (sometimes seductive) electro-acoustic rubbish.

Thus many of the more sensitive musicians quickly realized that it was as easy as it was superfluous to produce new sounds that were not the product of musical thought, just as it's easy nowadays to develop and "improve" the technologies of electronic music when these are devoid of any real and profound *raison d'être*. With or without new resources, electronic music had arrived at an *impasse* as a way of thinking musically. Indeed, these new resources had further detached it from a global idea of the musical work, understood not only from the technical, historical and expressive points of view, but also from the immediate and social ones. It was recognized, for example, that the spectacle of a public gathered together to listen to loudspeakers was not a particularly cheerful one, and that, yet again, the experience of public musical listening was made up of many different conventions, and was rooted in many different aspects of social and cultural life: it was not made up merely of a piece, a musical object to listen to, even if it proposed "new sounds". By its very nature, a piece of music by itself cannot easily transform listening conventions and socio-musical relations in general. Electronic music no longer seemed to have a definable and necessary destination . . . For his part, the musician sensed that a magnetic tape or interconnections on a synthesizer (in all their fragility and transience – and, indeed, their total detachment from the customary gestures of musical work) were not ideal "containers" for thought that had been elaborated in terms of survival and duration, precisely because it was thought. Not that one must let oneself become teutonically preoccupied with posterity, but undoubtedly the conviction that thought is permanent, that ideas have a longer life than things, and that men transmit ideas between them as durably as they transmit languages, is ingrained and implicit in human existence. Bertolt Brecht was fond of old objects that carried traces of the hands that had used them. I'm fond of them too, but on condition that the traces, and the form of the object, tell me something about the thought, the language and the function of those hands and that object. The idea of a musical thought preserved in the electromagnetic "memory" of a tape or in the digital memory of a computer, without any real contact with the specific nature of musical work, still poses problems, and will continue to do so until all the "parameters" – musical, scientific, technological, econ-omic and social – find a meeting-point, and achieve a sort of agreement.

D: Why do you think it is that this has not already come about in electronic music?

B: It's still true today, above all with the new technologies, that input is more important than output: thus it's still more useful to employ a digital system for its ability to transform sound data that are already established than for its ability to produce "new sounds". It's easy to produce new sounds: but to make these sounds the emanation of new musical thought, as happened in the Fifties, is for the moment more difficult. New musical thought, above all if it wants to manifest itself through new resources, must incorporate an awareness of musical experiences that are not new. There's no use in comparing a computer directing a digital system and a conductor directing an orchestra. The new technologies need above all to get closer to the work of performers, to find a place within it and extend it, rather than opposing themselves to it. It's not something that we ever really take proper account of, but however much today's concert-going public may have grown and become diversified, there remains latent within it a tenuous image of that very restrictive, selective and competent pre-romantic public (a public, that is, of enlightened dilettantes) which was also a potential performer of the music to which it listened – a public that judged music in terms that included their personal technical ability to master it, play it, and measure themselves musically (and privately) against it. Electronic music, with its advanced technologies and its emporium of new sounds and new acoustic necessities seemed intent upon administering a *coup de grace* to that tenuous image, that *alter Duft* from the distant past. But that's not what has happened, not only because you can expect too much from electronic music, but also because the new technologies can indeed make a concrete contribution to the world of voices and instruments – a different but perhaps also a deeper one. I think the time will soon be ripe to take creative advantage of today's researches, and thus to produce "works".

D: So it's the lack of socially accepted norms that damages electronic music, the fact that it wants to insert itself into a pre-existing situation as an alternative to it, without accepting its conditions of existence. Yet despite those difficulties there are works, including some of your own, that have gone beyond the phase of syntactical "experimentation".

B: Certainly there are, above all among the works of the Fifties and Sixties. There is in any case one aspect of "syntax" – electronic or otherwise – that has always interested me: that of redundancy. The absence of musical syntax (which can only be compensated for by utopian imagination and courage) also implies an absence of redundancy, if only because one of the functions of syntax is to let us anticipate, and to confirm what formally we already know. The new techniques and sounds of electronic music are particularly deprived of redundancy, not only because they don't make any reference to previously experienced models of behaviour and listening, nor even to familiar acoustic models, but also because there's no visible object or instrument producing the sounds, and you can't imagine anybody doing so either. When working with electronic music I've always tried to confront the problem of redundancy, not so much to induce anticipation of the next event or, every so often, to frustrate that anticipation (as normally happens in spoken language and "linguistic" music), but rather to make sure that every event, every sound process, should be bathed in sense: in other words, that it's given a "local" sense that refers to other senses in different temporal dimensions. The most elementary form of redundancy is repetition; it's often used as a stylistic cypher or, in its more obsessive forms – when the repeated elements are themselves insignificant – to ward off falling into meaningless disarray. Redundancy and repetition have some-times been at the centre of my preoccupations even outside electronic music: in certain parts of *Epifanie*, for example, and perhaps more than anywhere else in *Circles* (1960). In this piece I had tried to develop criteria of repetition that would involve all aspects of the composition; in fact in *Circles* everything repeats, and everything tends to turn back on itself, (including cumming's poems, naturally), whilst certain particular periodic character-istics tend to reverberate and to propagate themselves throughout the entire work. It must be a benign wink from the gods, or more probably just the law of large numbers, but even the copyright number printed on the score is circular, turns back on itself, and faithfully illustrates the use of cumming's three poems in the five movements that make up *Circles:* 13231.

But as I was saying earlier on, it's above all in the electronic works, and particularly those that combine live performance with sonic developments emerging from loudspeakers, that I have concerned myself with redundancy – though not necessarily as more or less periodic repetition. Take two works that are very distant from each other in time but share a common direction of research: *Différences* (for five instruments and tape), and *Chemins V* (for clarinet and programmed digital filters). Both are "French" in that the first was written for the "Domaine musicale" (Boulez conducted it in March, 1959) and the second for IRCAM. *Différences* was the first attempt to develop a relationship in depth between an instrumental group and the possibilities of electro-acoustics; with *Chemins V*, on the other hand, I want to make the performance of a clarinet solo interact with the programmed functions of a digital filter. To realize the tape for *Différences* (at the *Studio di fonologia musicale* in Milan) I began by recording in Paris, with the same musicians that would perform the piece in public just over a year later, sections for solo instruments or for different combinations of the five (flute, clarinet, harp, viola and cello). Whereas to realize *Chemins V*, I programmed, with the help of Vito Asta, instantaneous transformations of the sound of the clarinet. Thus, when performing *Différences*, a magnetic tape is synchronized with the five instruments playing on stage, while for *Chemins V* there's no tape recorder, but a digital system (Peppino di Giugno's famous 4X, realized at IRCAM), a little computer and converters. In *Différences* the original model of the five instruments coexists alongside an image of itself that is continually modified, until the *different* phases of transformation deliver up a completely altered image that no longer has anything to do with the original model. Whereas in *Chemins V*, the range of transformations through which the original model goes is much reduced: a clarinet is accompanied by its vocalized shadow. But the timing of the transformations is varied: the programme does not merely transform what the clarinet is playing at that moment, but also segments of what it played earlier, which were recorded in digital form. In *Différences* the tape is fixed once and for all; but in *Chemins V* what comes out of the microphones depends on the clarinettist's performance, which can influence the overall result in direct and immediate fashion. Finally, in *Différences* redundancy is guaranteed at several levels: every further transformational phase (there are five of them) always departs from (and returns to) a maximum of identity and fusion with the musical characteristics being developed by the instrumental group on stage. On the other hand, the instrumental group follows, provokes and confirms, as best it may, the electro-acoustic transformations on the tape, which thus acquires in part the function of a distorting mirror: it deforms and transforms the density of the instrumental group, it transforms the extension and speed of articulation, the intensity, the harmonic characteristics, and thus the acoustic properties of the ensemble. There's a sort of implicit musical dramaturgy in the different transformational phases, and in the continually varying relations between performance and recording. So I understand how Pousseur, to whom the piece is dedicated, can hear in *Différences* a scene from the Commedia dell'Arte, with the various alternating characters squabbling with one another, putting on masks, taking them off again, etc. I understand, even though I don't share his view. The progress of *Différences*, firmly anchored to the five instruments on stage, is made up of two simultaneous developments, in different dimensions, of the same material. In *Chemins V,* on the other hand, redundancy is originally provided by the long melody for solo clarinet which leads the piece through a series of homogeneous situations. It's a real melody, with its own hierarchy of intervals, symmetries, repetitions, with rather precise expressive characteristics and, indeed, its redundancies. I said earlier that the clarinet is often accompanied by its own vocalized shadow: imposed on the sound of the clarinet are privileged points of resonance, which are neither uniform nor static, and thus resemble the points of resonance that, in phonation, characterize and define vocal sounds. These are the bands of reinforced resonance, the formants, that permit us to recognize vowel sounds when they are pronounced by different people, and that make life difficult for singers when they want to make words comprehensible while singing in extreme registers.

D: What are the aims of IRCAM – the Institut de recherche et de coordination acoustique-musique *in Paris?*

B: Now that I've rather detached myself from IRCAM, it's not so easy to define them. In a different epoch, it could have become Boulez's Bayreuth, but today there are many reasons why that would have made no sense – among them, the essential purity and modernity of Boulez's thought. IRCAM's original aims are expressed in its own name, and I think they're correct and far-seeing: the attempt to give a new musical sense to applied acoustic research and today's technologies, and the attempt to find an acoustically and technologically new formulation for musical thought. All this without wanting to establish causal relationships between music and technology, at least on the technical level, since we shall otherwise find ourselves discussing chickens and eggs. However, it's certainly true that Boulez tends to think that, for example, architecture has changed because of glass and steel and that, by analogy, music ought to change because of new technologies, computers, etc. In fact, when he talks about electronic music, Boulez tends to forget its history: he seems *furiously* impelled to forget the realizations of Stockhausen and others (myself included). Whereas I continue to believe that it was architectural thought, with its vast range of determinations and functions, that took notice of glass and steel, just as it was musical thought, at the start of the Fifties, that took notice of oscillators and sound generators in general, which were already there in any case, just as glass and steel were there for architects. The relationship between these machines and musical thought is certainly fascinating, but it's neither easy nor obvious. I reckon that for some time yet that relationship will only be resolved anecdotally, that is, with works that here and there throw new and original light on the relationship, but that don't define a line of conduct overall, in other words, don't place themselves within an aesthetic and, as it were, universal perspective.

The composer who works with the new resources of electronic music (computers included) tends by the nature of things to put his past on one side, and do something *different* and exceptional, though he risks momentarily losing track of the deeper nexus and the continuity of his musical decisions, and of his own presence. It's certainly no accident that the most interesting works produced with the new digital technologies are by musicians without a past (not out of choice, but through age or simply lack of musical awareness; it's likewise no accident that the most significant realizations in electronic music (such as Stockhausen's) are still those that make use of hybrid, open electro-acoustic systems that are ready for anything. Perhaps the most dramatic and interesting aspect of IRCAM is precisely the search for a necessary relationship between the most advanced technologies and musical thought, a musical thought that, to be such, must perforce have roots a long way away from the technologies that attract it. You sometimes get the impression that musicians let themselves be chosen by the new technologies, without being able to establish, dialectically, a relationship of real and profound necessity. One can, in fact, move indifferently from one system to another, from one calculator to another (they are always faster, more sophisticated, powerful, and they are always smaller) without having really musically used what one had before. Technological developments (and also certain industrial interests) tend, by their very nature, to be indifferent to musical concerns and prefer to follow the law of technology and of the market, which is that of always, and at all costs making things better: and the musician seems to think that things are better only if he has at his disposition more sophisticated resources. The fact is that the initial thrust towards better resources has to spring initially from a musical conception, and it's only starting from this that you can get a profitable and detailed exchange between music and technology going.

In music, as I find myself forever saying, things don't get better or worse: they evolve and transform themselves. It is often we ourselves who are incapable of taking in the nexus of those transformations, and we ourselves, again, who sometimes fail to look in the direction of the highest and best part of ourselves and our surroundings ... When a musical or para-musical tool improves, the reasons aren't necessarily musical ones. Behind a better computer for music stands not IRCAM and its musicians, but the banks, the airports, the police, the Stock Exchange, medicine, NASA and, naturally, the electronics and computer industries. It's because of this that IRCAM's most interesting technical and scientific achievements are those developed by Peppino Di Giugno. They are doubly interesting because they make no ingenuous attempts to be super-instruments (as do commercial synthesizers), nor are they linked to the fashion for better computers: in fact, they are themselves extra-rapid computers conceived exclusively for musical use, and not to book an air ticket. In relation to known musical instruments, these machines of Di Giugno's (which are open, neutral systems, to be redefined each time they are used) seem a bit like foundlings, lacking as they do a genetic history that can be recognized in terms of musical experience: they have to learn everything, they have to learn to live many different lives musically. And this is precisely one of the most important functions of IRCAM – "educating" the new resources, and anchoring them to musical reality in all of its many aspects. It's not an easy thing to do. Just as it's not easy to use and develop creatively one of the most muscially important aspects of the new digital technologies in general: that of being able to control with equal finesse the *microscopic* temporal dimension (which is not perceived as such, and is measured in milliseconds), the global, *macroscopic* dimension (which brings into play the different levels of our memory) and, finally, the intermediate dimension, that of perceptible durations, rhythmic articulation, and even on occasion melodies ... To create, to programme a muscially coherent and significant relationship between these three dimensions would mean, as far as I'm concerned, taking a step forward in the conquest of a wider musical space. In recent years we have all tested the musical limits of technicians, and now it seems to me that we are about to test the technical limits of musicians. And there's nothing wrong with that. On the contrary, it is precisely in the slow, tiring search for a convergence and (always rather utopian) identification between science and music that new things are found, and one can hope to carry on creatively coordinating acoustic and musical dimensions. One of the problems of IRCAM as a place for creating things is perhaps that it is too big, and it sometimes seems to be subject to Parkinson's Law as applied in public administration (non-correspondence between the energy and tempo of work, and the work actually produced), while Boulez is often obliged to behave like a captain of industry. The very conflict that was predicted when IRCAM came into being, and they tried to celebrate a sumptuous and rather rushed marriage between science and music, is now reflected in many aspects of the Institute's life.

However, one of the most interesting and sane aspects of IRCAM is its mobility and its flexible structure: at one time it was rather artificially divided into five departments, whereas now it's divided into two blocks (one scientific, the other artistic). It will certainly try out other forms of organization in the future. But one thing is certain, and that is that IRCAM is in the most intelligent and restless hands that you can imagine: those of Pierre Boulez. It's thanks to him that IRCAM is not only identified with what goes on underground – a space perhaps inhabited by too many "Leporellos" and too many potential "Cosimas" – but also with its relationship to the outside world, and the problems that this relationship entails. And then there are the concert activities of the Ensemble Intercontemporain, which are a high-quality bridge out to musical life *"en plein air"*. I've conducted them myself, and they are marvellous performers.

D: How does your work as an orchestral conductor link up with your work as a composer? I get the impression that you don't often conduct works by other composers.

B: That's right, I don't, because I'm not a "professional" conductor. And anyway, I don't want to conduct a great deal because I enjoy travelling less and less. From 1970 to 1977 I spent my life in hotels. Nowadays there are more concerts that I decide not to conduct than those I do. I've never really been interested in a conducting career: I'm simply a composer who conducts. But perhaps that "simply" is out of place because I am handicapped as a conductor by the fact that, psychologically speaking, I'm not a *performer*. I get enormous pleasure out of working with musicians but, if it were up to me, after the last rehearsal I could almost do without the concert. It must be a form of egoism. Imagine my state of prostration when I conduct in Israel, where every one of the Philharmonic's programmes have to be repeated seven, eight, even nine times in an auditorium holding 3000 people, given the excessive number of subscribers. Anyway, I prefer to direct my own works because I think I know them better than anyone else, and am able to give the clearest and most legible account of them.

D: But are you sure that Beethoven would conduct his symphonies better than von Karajan?

B: That was an epoch in which the conductor had a different function and a different relation with his musicians. Indeed, it was at precisely that time, at the beginning of the last century, that the figure of the orchestral conductor began to define itself. But conditions were so different then, from every point of view, that comparisons are impossible. Just think that Beethoven conducted the *Third* and *Fourth* Symphonies with an orchestra of about 30 musicians! And think how the *Violin Concerto* was first performed, if I'm not mistaken: without conductor, and with the leader playing the solo part and giving the tempo to the orchestra. The performances of a modern orchestra with 90 players are almost transcriptions when compared with the conditions that prevailed then: not that there's anything wrong with that – on the contrary. Several years ago, when I was working on the television programme *"C'è musica e musica"*, I allowed myself the satisfaction of recording part of the *Third Symphony* with the same number of players that Beethoven used (29). I was afraid that the different quality and power of the sound from woodwind and brass would alter the orchestral equilibrium, especially in the *fortissimi*. But it didn't. It was an unforgettable experience to hear an *Eroica* as transparent and well-defined as chamber music. Extremely dilated and explosive chamber music, naturally. But to return to myself: Maderna conducted my works better than I could have done; for example he conducted *Nones* and *Allelujah II* as though he'd written them himself. Boulez conducted my *Concerto* for two pianos and orchestra better than I did; the same is true of Abbado's version of *Il ritorno degli Snovidenia* and Lorin Maazel's version of *Coro*. But saying "better" is not perhaps quite right. As a composer, I inevitably tend to create for myself habits and hierarchies of listening (particularly as concerns the emphasizing of certain details) which don't necessarily coincide with the more objective and homogeneous (but not necessarily "correct") vision of another, technically perfect conductor. But it gives me a surprise, and if I find it attractive I can even change my mind, modify my listening hierarchies, and be deeply grateful to Boulez, Abbado or Maazel for having revealed to me a slightly different version of my work. I suppose the same thing must have happened to Stravinsky when, in his later years, he heard Boulez conducting *Le Sacre*.

D: Have you ever felt misrepresented or misunderstood by the press?

B: Often enough. But it's perfectly natural, and I don't pay much attention unless the critic is someone whom I also greatly admire as a non-critic. It's a dreadful job being a critic because it's uncertain and incomplete: I don't see the musical, cultural or even social usefulness of someone who has to write articles every week for the dailies or weeklies, and does *nothing else*. In their place I'd go mad after a fortnight. When I go to a concert and hear a Schubert sonata for the nth time, marvellously interpreted by Pollini or Brendel, I sometimes wonder in dismay what on earth I would write if I were a critic and wanted to avoid the usual panegyrics, the usual fountain of useless words. Who knows, I'd probably end up doing the same thing as everyone else to avoid going hungry. But I wonder whether in the long run a profession of that sort, always concentrated on other people's work, always busy giving judgement on what other people are doing (other people of today, not yesterday) doesn't end up damaging your intellectual and moral fibre. It's no accident that the pillars of Italian musical criticism – undoubtedly the best that I've ever come across – are people deeply rooted in musical work and history, outside their activity as music critics. As well as exporting to the United States luxury goods, spaghetti and university lecturers, Italy ought to export (only temporarily, mind you) a few music critics. Imagine what an impression it would leave, and what beneficent confusion it would create if you let Fedele D'Amico write for the New York Times even for a single month (assuming that he'd allow himself to be exported).

As I was saying, the critic's job is an uncertain and fragile one, and I suppose that it's because of that that even esteemed and refined scholars – overcome by the boredom of their semi-profession – sometimes permit themselves the most unforgive-able forms of spitefulness, so as to amuse themselves a little and make their young friends laugh. I think that criticism can be useful when it knows how to criticize itself. But it's so difficult! Real criticism, which doesn't confine itself to little weekly articles, thus has its own autonomy, its own history, its own "poetics" and therefore its own needs. For example, a really intelligent and creative critic can develop and theorize a line of argument that is speculative and partially independent of reality, and will then look for confirmation of his arguments in musical reality. It may be that reality will offer him little proof; it may even be that nobody and no music can give him the evidence that he's looking for. Then he becomes like a scientist with no starting point for his inductions, a voice crying in the wilderness, a Nietzschean metaphor. And then the critic invents for himself the proofs that he needs, and since by professional habit he normally has little patience, and the future doesn't interest him or makes him suspicious, he invests in works and musicians more than they can effectively contain and express. These are the cases of misplaced trust, where the critical vision as a whole pitches itself at an intellectually and creatively superior level to the works that ought to substantiate it. But there's nothing seriously wrong in all this, nor can anything dramatic really occur because in the end, as we all know, in the exercise of musical criticism – as in nature – nothing is created and nothing is *really* destroyed.

D: Casting a quick eye back over thirty years of work, do you find throughout that period the image of music which you proposed at the start of our interview – that is, a music that establishes harmony between the practical and spiritual spheres of the individual?

B: So here we are back to the first question. And so we should be. But I didn't mean to attribute that idea of music to my own activities alone, but rather to all music, and to everyone's activities: creators, interpreters, listeners, and even those who don't know anything about music. In fact it's not only an idea of music. The concept of an understanding, an "intelligent" relation – in other words a harmony – between the sphere of the body and the senses on one hand, and the intellectual and spiritual sphere on the other is a very general one. So general and universal that it is present, as a binary opposition, in any human behaviour: the language that we speak, the morals that we accept, the computer that we use and the music that we make. We're pervaded with binary oppositions: *positive* and *negative, heaven* and *earth, man* and *woman,* Sanguineti's *"senses* and *speculative grammar",* *yes* and *no, dominant* and *tonic, raw* and *cooked, vowels* and *consonants.* It's not my job to discuss dualism and duality: the mediaeval philosophers have already done it, as have contemporary mathematicians – and anyway, I don't need to demonstrate what I do in words. I just mean that the terms of binary oppositions are complementary and that, taken separately, granted that we were able to do so, they become abstract. It's rather like Jacobson's famous phonological classifications made up of binary oppositions between vowel and non-vowel sounds, etc., and between different phonemes that are in themselves abstract entities and exist only as differential qualities within a system of oppositions. For me acting musically means making complementary or harmonizing the terms of an opposition or a group of oppositions – making them concrete, that is. The relation between practical and spiritual spheres in music is obvious, if only because it demands ears, fingers, consciousness and intellect. But both spheres are in turn inhabited by innumerable oppositions, not necessarily symmetrical ones, which are not so much the emanation of a methodology (such as Jakobson's phonology) as of a historical and expressive musical reality. For me, music is giving a sense to the passage between the differing terms of an opposition, and between different oppositions, inventing a relationship between them and making one opposition speak with the voice of the other – as when the body speaks with the voice of the mind and vice versa. So arranging things, in other words, that the elements of the oppositions become part of a single thing. It interests me to place those elements further and further away from each other, so far away that the search for a complementarity and unity between them becomes a very dangerous and complex operation.

D: Why dangerous?

B: Because between those distant points (between an African hetrophony and myself, for example, or between one harmonic dimension and another) you may find the whole history of music and, unless you're going to pretend that there's nothing there and stick your head in the sand, this implies a continual shifting of perspective that can take you momentarily off course. Consciousness of history implies movement, both inside and outside ourselves; and history doesn't stand still in our ears either. And it seems to me that it's within this perspective of mobility and risk that the very consciousness of musical time as *quality* in continual development becomes a representation of the consciousness of history. I don't believe in poetics of immobility. And then the sense of danger and even holocaust pervades almost everything these days. There is a great deal of mystery around us. Romantic man was surrounded by a mysterious and impassive nature. Today, man is surrounded by an equally mysterious and substantially malign culture; a culture that, both on a planetary and a local level, often presents itself as a very unstable and dangerous emulsion of transformations, oppressions, and (often mishandled) skirmishes – with few prospects of an amalgam. So let's end our interview on music here, and may I just say that if this emulsion one day "precipitates" and explodes, we should at least be able to offer – to those that come after us God knows how, and God knows from where – real and historically responsible things and not false things, unworthy of memory. And that, in the long run, is what music has always done, in good times as in bad . . .

INTERVIEW 1

with Bálint András Varga

Varga: You have always been much involved with the human voice: when was it that you first began to experiment with it?

Berio: It was my experience with the electronic work *Thema (Omaggio a Joyce)* that first drew my attention to the new possibilities inherent in the human voice. In electronic music we make no distinction between human and instrumental sound: we use sound as an acoustical phenomenon regardless of its origin. Superficially, it might appear as though this would deprive it of an important characteristic – its meaning. In reality, however, exactly the opposite is the case: when analyzed, new strata of meaning come to the surface.

V: But for all that, in your vocal works you always use words, and employ vocal effects very rarely. In A-Ronne *breathing, sighing and other noises do become part of the musical process, and* Sequenza III *is another exception. But such elements are missing in most of your vocal compositions.*

B: I am not interested in sound by itself – and even less in sound effects, whether of vocal or instrumental origin. I work with words because I find new meaning in them by analyzing them acoustically and musically. I rediscover the word. As far as breathing and sighing are concerned, these are not effects but vocal gestures which also carry a meaning: they must be considered and perceived in their proper context.

A-Ronne is built entirely of stereotypes, of sounds that you can hear any day. And the text by Edoardo Sanguineti is a sequence of quotations. From a certain point of view it is a poem – I repeat it many times, emphasizing some of its lines, suggesting new meanings and new associations. Even if I treat the words neutrally in places, dismissing their meaning, the presence and the use of that particular poem is fundamental: The telephone directory would not have been suitable, even though I think it is important, occasionally, to suggest a certain indifference in relation to a text, to keep a certain musical distance from it.

The "grammar" of *A-Ronne* is focussed on a single technique: alliteration. It is with the help of alliteration that I musically reorganize this rather complex text.

V: It is built around three subjects: beginning, middle and end.

B: Yes, and it is mostly heard in two or three languages. It was specially written by Edoardo Sanguineti. It was our only joint venture which was not the outcome of a long process of maturing and of constant dialogue and consultation. I told him over the telephone what I had in mind – short sentences which can be taken apart into small segments – and after two days I received from Sanguineti this beautiful text.

V: The friendship of Edoardo Sanguineti and Umberto Eco, the influence of their ideas and works have considerably affected your own composition over more than two and a half decades.

B: Yes, both of them have played an important role in my life. I met Eco in Milan in the mid-fifties. We soon discovered that we took a similar interest in poetry and within it, onomatopoeia: I introduced him to linguistics and he introduced me to Joyce. I met Sanguineti through him: when I was thinking about *Passaggio*, Eco suggested that I should contact him. Sanguineti did in fact add a new dimension to the piece: he called my attention to the figure of Rosa Luxemburg (whereas I was mainly thinking of Milena, the addressee of Kafka's letters) and eventually he wrote the text of the work.

Without Eco *Thema (Omaggio a Joyce)* wouldn't exist. Both of us were fascinated by onomatopoeia in poetry and after having gone through Italian literature, we addressed ourselves to Joyce. The eleventh chapter of *Ulysses* is a triumph of onomatopoeia. Joyce employs a different technique in each chapter and since this one is devoted to music, his musical reference is the fuga per canonem. This is of course impossible to realize with a written text, in the original sense of the term: it is a kind of generalized metaphor. But even so there is a subject, a counter-subject, a development, there are stretti – and different performing techniques, too, such as trills, glissandi, and so on. We only concentrated on the beginning of the chapter (the exposition of the fugue), up to the "cadenza" where everything becomes saturated by *s*, a kind of cadence of white noise. We then compared the sound of the English text with those of the French and Italian translations.

V: Why do that?

B: Poetry has always looked at music nostalgically – as though at an unattainable possibility. The associative mechanism of poetry tends to suppress the musical character of its sound. I was interested in how to bridge the distance between poetry and music.

Eco and I copied the English, French and Italian readings of Ulysses so that the onomatopoeic sections overlapped. At such places tension grew to the point of explosion.

That kind of research was gradually replaced by music. The aim of *Thema (Omaggio a Joyce)* was to create a genuine composition by making use of the material of words, so that we don't know any more whether what we hear is poetry or music. At the end, words and poetry take over once again.

V: The different stages of preparing Thema *were described by you in a long article. It was a highly complex, multifaceted job. Obviously, your experience with electronic music helped you a lot.*

B: Of course. First of all, I defined the key points of the text. In vocal music, a great deal has to be sacrificed, destroyed because we cannot control everything. This was obvious also in the preparatory phase of *Thema*. After selecting the material, I linked the words according to their acoustical properties rather than simply their order of occurrence. After that, I connected them according to their meaning. In other words, I established an acoustical and a semantic frame and then transformed the words alternately according to the requirements of one or the other, with various technical means, most of them perhaps rudimentary: complicated editing, filters, acceleration, slowing down etc.

V: Thema (Omaggio a Joyce) *was at the same time a lesson for later works.*

B: Certainly. *Thema* was of basic significance in my work because through it I experienced the text not as a closed, unchangeable object but as one whose meaning and sound both allow the proliferation of new functions. *Circles,* written two years later, is in many ways related to the basic idea of *Thema.* Here, too, I worked with an English text – three poems by e.e. cummings which form a transition from the simple to the complex. I did not write a piece for solo voice with instrumental accompaniment, but rather one where there is a very strong connection between the phonetic quality of the text and the musical texture. The poems generate or determine innumerable musical events and the vocal part often seems to be generated by the instrumental ones. That is how I was able to explore the intrinsic quality of the poetry. The musical material was so complex that I felt I had to return to the same poems a second time, in the following order: 1-2-3-2-1. However, the second time round the second poem is linked to musical material from the first setting of the first poem.

V: Circles *is indeed a unique alloy of music and poetry. I felt while listening to it that the music influenced the poetry, gave it a new meaning and raised it on to a different plain.*

B: That was precisely my objective. Sometimes the visual aspect of the cummings poems reminds me of a battlefield, you could also say that different elements of the words copulate with one another to form new words. It is all very expressive and forceful, and naturally it conditions the musical realization.

I grouped the instruments around the text, reflecting the phonetic families so that the sound is sometimes short-circuited and explodes.

V: What is the significance of the singer walking from one instrumental group to another?

B: That is how she forms an ever closer contact with the instruments. At the beginning of the piece, she stands on her own, with the instruments behind her, almost merely accompanying her. Subsequently, her part becomes more and more merged with the instrumental material, and this has to be reflected on an acoustical level as well. At the end of the piece, the percussionists are also singing. That is how it comes full circle: the four performers become one.

V: Is that the explanation of the title?

B: Not just that. Everything in the piece is circular: the use of the text, the sequence of certain sounds, etc.

V: Could one describe certain parts of Circles *as aleatoric?*

B: No, it is true that at one point the percussionists have to play on all the instruments around them as fast as possible. But I wanted to achieve a particular effect with that, and since percussion instruments can be treated in a less specific way than the violin, cello or clarinet, it would make no sense to tie the hands of the performers too much. It is better to leave them a certain physical freedom and only to lay down the general direction of their action. Otherwise we would paralyse them. There is no question of aleatoricism, however.

V: Why do you reject it?

B: Because in my opinion it is like cheating the listener, since he has no part in the aleatory process. The audience has no choice, it has to listen to whatever is put before it, aleatory or not. Furthermore, aleatoricism means that the composer renounces certain responsibilities.

All of this reminds me of Brecht. He did not understand traditional opera and made simple-minded statements about it, especially about the works of Mozart. Nevertheless, he was right to a certain extent when he said that if somebody dies, it is a very serious thing. But if somebody is singing while he dies it is grotesque: in order for it not to be, the audience would have to be singing too. In our case in order for it not to be "grotesque", the audience should also be able to participate in the chance machinery, in the open possibilities of open sound events . . .

In the end, I do not believe in chance as far as music is concerned. It is simply a deception. The musical process is so complex that even if the composer doesn't want to suggest or impose any intentionality, the performer will do it in his place.

V: Let us return to your vocal compositions and Umberto Eco. Epifanie *is an important work of the early sixties, both in its significance and its dimensions. I understand that you selected its texts partly on the advice of Eco.*

B: Before talking about *Epifanie,* maybe I should mention *Visage* where, rather as in *Circles,* I attempted to transform the basic connotations of the human voice by relating it to - and extending it into - similar sound families electronically produced. I worked at it for one year and meant it to be a radio composition. The recording was made with Cathy Berberian; she performed vocal gestures - for instance, characteristic English and Hebrew intonations, the inflections of television speech, of Neapolitan dialect, and so on. The vocal gestures were not transformed electronically, but constantly related to, and were commented upon by electronically produced sound families. To start with I was thinking of *Visage* as a soundtrack for an imaginery drama. Instead, it turned out to be a highly complex work which is rather difficult to label.

As far as the text of *Epifanie* is concerned, Eco's most important suggestion was to make the order of the quotations inter-changeable within certain limits. The result should always suggest a process or development, if you like - based not only on the music but also on the content of the poems used. It can, for instance, start with Proust and end with Brecht; in other words, it can start out from a distant, complex and almost decadent poetic image and reach its opposite – for after all, the Brecht is like a kick in the stomach. If the order is changed, the relationship between literature and reality is explored in a more round-about way and of course the musical process is also changed. The literary quotations – more than half of which were suggested by Eco – have an image in common: the tree. It can be regarded as a tribute to Brecht who, in his famous poem *An die Nachgeborenen* which is used in "Epifanie", reminds us of those hard times when talking about trees becomes a sin because it means keeping silent about tragedies and injustices.

V: For the recording of Epifanie, *you selected the first of the nine possible orders.*

B: Yes, that is the one I like most. The possibilities are also based on musical considerations: there is a harmonic alliteration between the end of one piece and the beginning of another – in other words, the same thing is continued in a different context.

V: Do you like the original version, too, where the three Quaderni *are performed without the vocal part?*

B: I have not heard it for a long time. *Epifanie* is the one that I feel closest to. We can actually regard the piece as two cycles – one vocal, one orchestral – which are performed simultaneously. The vocal cycle appears as an epiphany, that is, as a kind of sudden apparition, in the more complex orchestral texture.

V: The title and perhaps the very notion of the epiphany were presumably suggested by Joyce, who explains its meaning in his Portrait of the Artist as a Young Man.*?*

B: That's right. The *Portrait* suggested one of the episodes in *Epifanie*, too; the apparition of the girl who is like a sea-bird.

V: The music of that episode is like a folk song – it is very erotic, very human, while the vocal writing of some of the other movements seems to me rather neutral, almost synthetic.

B: *Epifanie* is a very diversified work. The "vocal cycle" in particular covers a wide range of vocal expressions, and techniques. By comparison the "orchestral cycle" is very unified.

V: Why do you use the nota battuta *in the Joyce episode?*

B: For descriptive and expressive reasons, the subject being a "girl-bird": you could call it a "madrigalism". But also because that technqiue has fallen into oblivion, as have so many others: I taught it to Cathy and she mastered it extremely well.

V: The folk-song-like intonation of two movements in Epifanie *anticipates the increased role of folk music in some of your later works:* Folk Songs *and, on another level,* Cries of London *and* Coro.

B: My links with folk music are often of an emotional character. When I work with that music, I am always caught by the thrill of discovery.

V: In Folk Songs *you must have tried to retain the authenticity of the original folk songs (except, of course, for those which are not folk melodies).*

B: No, I did not have that in mind. I am interested in taking possession of that treasure with my own means. I return again and again to folk music because I try to establish contact between that and my own ideas about music. I have a Utopian dream, though I know it cannot be realized: I would like to create a unity between folk music and our music – a real, perceptible, understandable continuity between ancient, popular music-making which is so close to everyday work and our music.

I am no ethnomusicologist but sometimes I wish I were able to devote more time to research. Yet it is not my intention to preserve the authenticity of a folk song. My transcriptions are analyses of folk songs and at the same time convey the flavour of that music as I see it.

V: Nevertheless, in Folk Songs *you mostly start out from genuine folk music while your other folk-inspired compositions do not use original melodies. In* Cries of London, *for instance, you do not quote the cries of street vendors in their original form.*

B: *Cries of London* consists of archetypes. It is like a naive painting, or rather a series of naive paintings, each of which has its very precise and simple character.

V: I know that you prefer the version for eight singers but I feel that the first one, written for the six soloists of the King's Singers, is much more authentic and "popular". The new version is less direct.

B: The new version contains some more songs and there is also a last cry which is like a comment on the others. I treat the rest as though they were written by other people and I only found them, while the last one, the comment, is really mine. In other words, I look at the cries from a certain distance and step back into myself only in the last one.

V: I was interested to read that in 1968 you went to Sicily to record some folk songs.

B: Yes, I spent a month and a half in Sicily and wrote much of *Sinfonia* there. Sometimes I would get together with musicologists and also folk singers. I remember with special pleasure Celano, who has since died. He was a remarkable story-teller – he could tell tales for days on end, sometimes sang, and he spoke in a rhythmical manner marking the beat with his feet. He even had a sword and beat the rhythm with it. He had an astonishing singing technique which enabled him to sing all the *abbagnate*. That is what the cries of Sicilian street vendors are called. On one part of the island, the people who sell oranges, melons and fish all sing differently; some melodies are so beautiful that one would think they were love songs. In the past, the vendors even arranged contests to see who could sing best. Celano introduced me to these tunes and I recorded them on tape. Much later they gave me the idea of writing *Cries of London* which, of course, has nothing to do with those of Sicily.

V: Did anyone collect abbagnate before you?

B: Yes. Several conventionally notated Sicilian anthologies for voice and piano have been published. Their harmonization is at times arbitrary, but they were done by a musician with a sensitive ear – Favara. In their way, his arrangements are much more valuable than those of Marie Joseph Canteloube who, in his *Chants d'Auvergne*, manipulated the original songs in a silly and offensive manner.

V: Among your folk-inspired compositions, Coro *is the one on the largest scale, both in its musical material and its dimensions.*

B: Yes, and at the same time it is related to many of my earlier works – strangely enough even to *Epifanie* which, as I said, is actually two cycles, one orchestral the other vocal. In *Coro*, instead, one "cycle" is based on writings by Pablo Neruda, the other on different texts of folk origin. The two appear alternately in the composition: they merge together only at the end.

In *Coro* I do not quote folk melodies but I do use certain folk techniques and procedures which I link to completely different musical material. That is how I retain my freedom, and how I can switch from one to the other while retaining the individual features of an ethnic area.

Coro is also related to *Sinfonia* in that the human voice is often part of the orchestral sound. And, like *Coro, Sinfonia* also makes use of many different techniques.

In *Coro*, I do not use a chorus in the traditional sense of the word. I seat each of the forty singers next to an orchestral player, the two forming a pair. This solution has many reasons. The members of the chorus often sing solos or form groups of three or four. They are seated at different points on the podium to be heard to better advantage and, occasionally, to achieve a total fusion.

It is also in the interest of clear intonation that an orchestral player is sitting next to each singer – it allows me to divide the chorus into many independent parts. The multiple divisi of the voices and the instruments result in a special quality of sound.

V: Like the Concerto for two pianos *and* Tempi Concertati, *where the instruments conduct a dialogue with one another, there is a "conversation" in* Coro *between the vocal and instrumental parts. At the same time, you make no difference between vocal and instrumental sound and in this way the sonority becomes homogeneous.*

B: Yes, that reflects my attempt also to create an acoustical unity among different techniques and ways of music-making.

Coro is in actual fact a huge ballad, and like any other ballad it has a character, its own regularities and moods. Certain texts and harmonic fields recur several times but always generate different musical situations and "moods". There is a rotation and at the same time, a constant transformation of materials. Towards the end, when Pablo Neruda reminds us again and again of the blood in the street and the folk text is about love and work – that is, things that form the basis of our life – the two dimensions of the piece meet and become one.

V: I was powerfully impressed by the tragic mood of Coro. *It struck me as a kind of supra-national, non-liturgical requiem.*

B: I am reluctant to discuss the expressive aspect of my music in detail, but basically I agree. In the course of the piece contrasts gradually disappear, and merge into a single mood of dark suspension. *Coro* ends with a question mark.

V: Bartok's dream about the brotherhood of nations came to my mind.

B: I was not thinking of nations, but of the meeting of people, each with their own history, but with their different loves and homes destroyed. I must admit that there is a tragic mood in *Coro*. Maybe because of the constant re-emergence of certain words and melodies which gradually disappear, or are suddenly crushed or hidden. Yes, you can think of poor people, whose lives are too often destroyed. I had originally meant *Coro* to have a simple, expressive character. I thought of it as a musical transposition of the Italian Festival dell'Unità. I have been very attached to this annual summer festivity, filled with joy at the sense of community that it creates among the many guests who come for this occasion from various parts of the world. There is a lot of music, many discussions, a lot of food and a lot of happy, honest faces. Anyway,

I did keep from the original plan the idea of performing the piece on a podium with steps of different height so that the audience could see clearly all the singers and all the players. It is also necessary for acoustical reasons. But gradually the steps of that podium became in my mind the Odessa steps as we saw them in Eisenstein's film *The Battleship Potemkin*. In a way, *Coro* is my "Potemkin".

V: In accordance with Coro's *international character, you use several languages.*

B: I use five: Italian, French, English, Hebrew and German. The exotic languages appear in German translation.

V: You have mentioned that you use different folk performance techniques. How did you come across them – how did you study Central African singing techniques for instance?

B: An ethnomusicologist friend of mine, Simha Arom, has studied them. He spent months in Central Africa and even learned the language. He was surprised how a large crowd of people could sing or play the trumpet in a strict and complex counterpoint (though incidentally I would not call it counterpoint, but heterophony). Finally he understood that everybody was relating his part to a melody, similar to the tenor in old forms of counterpoint. However, the melody could not be heard, it was never played in that form, but was a hidden agreement, a kind of social contract. Arom eventually asked the natives to sing their parts one by one. He recorded them on tape and then superimposed the forty or fifty parts on top of one another – and reconstituted the original result.

V: It is like migrating birds who instinctively find the right direction.

B: Yes, it is astonishing. We have not got anything like it. Not that they are superior to us, because our music is much more complex. It is surprising as a psychological phenomenon, because they are capable of coordinating the tempo and not deviating from it.

In *Coro*, I have used that Central African technique but applied it to Yugoslav musical material. That is just one example of the way I try to create something completely different by linking playing techniques and melodies of different origins – and, in addition, I develop those techniques in a different direction.

V: Where did you come across Persian folk music?

B: A friend in Paris, Jean-Pierre Drouet, is an expert in Persian drumming. The poem I heard by chance on television – I liked it, and copied it down.

V: How about Yugoslav melodies?

B: I have lots and lots of books and records with Macedonian, Croatian and other Yugoslav folk music.

V: If you got as far as Yugoslavia, why didn't you go just a bit further north and use some Hungarian folk music?

B: Bartók did it before me and if I touched Hungarian folk music I would feel as if I were entering a sanctuary illegally. I am very attracted to the folk music of Eastern Europe (Bulgaria particularly) and I may well return to it one day in a different form.

V: You have said of Coro *that it is not finished – in theory it could be continued indefinitely.*

B: I simply meant that the additive nature of the work is such that I could have extended it for much longer. After all, dense and complex musical materials alternate with simpler ones. The complex episodes generate the simpler ones. The vocal solos often draw their part from the complex musical material that precedes them. It is rich enough to be "tapped" for more songs. At the same time, throughout the piece, there are constantly recurring elements.

V: I remember how fascinated I was when I heard Coro *at the Warsaw Autumn Festival by the movement of sound from one point of the podium to another, not to speak of the novelty of the sound. The relationship between physical space and sound was one of the basic experiences of the piece for me.*

The problem of space, however, interested you at the time of writing Perspectives. *It also played a role in* Allelujah II *as well as in* Circles *and perhaps* Passaggio.

B. I use space differently from piece to piece. In 1955 when writing *Allelujah* I placed five different instrumental groups on the podium but I came to the conclusion that they could not be heard separately. So I followed it up with *Allelujah II* where I altered the composition of the groups and placed them at different points in the hall. Groups containing similar instruments were placed as far apart as possible, while those with different instruments were seated closer to each other. Often, there is chamber music playing within a group or between the groups.

V. Were you interested in sound moving round the hall or diagonally?

B. Such things occur in order to call attention to the relationship between identical instruments in different groups. Groups one and five, for instance, have many brass instruments in common, and sometimes they play together. But tricks like moving the sound round and round the hall – easy solutions that Boulez calls car racing – don't interest me. The groups are in a hierarchical order. The most important instrument in *Allelujah II* is the flute and the most prominent note is *b* flat. It is round that pitch centre that related harmonic fields, constellations and structures rotate. The piece starts with that note and ends with it – it is sounded by the flute in the second instrumental group. The *b* flat is present practically throughout and serves as a kind of focal point amidst the complex and rather centrifugal musical processes.

Coro is different: here the role of space is determined by the relationship between the registers of the human voice and the instruments. For instance, I couple the sopranos with the flute, the violin and the oboe – in other words, with high instruments. I wanted to form a soprano territory, an alto territory, and so on, even if they are not completely isolated. Some of the basses are mixed with the sopranos and the altos are also mixed with the tenors and the basses. All of this requires a seating of the orchestra which differs from the traditional one. The range of the trumpets, for instance, is the same as that of the tenors and altos and the first trumpet plays together with a tenor, the second with an alto. One horn is also seated next to a tenor, while another sits with a bass. At the same time, I did not want to completely disperse voices of the same range because it would be dangerous if they lost contact with one another altogether.

V: Is Tempi concertati *organized along the same lines as* Allelujah II? *After all, it too consists of several instrumental groups.*

B: Almost. The two pianos are put in the groups furthest apart and so are the harps while the flute and the violin play masters of ceremony in the middle of the podium.

V: After these detours, let us return to the main subject of our conversation – vocal compositions, and amongst them, those works of yours inspired by folk music. I am afraid I have had no access to Questo vuol dire che *which seems to be a rather odd piece according to the descriptions I have read of it.*

B: It is not a composition, just a frame. It is also based on folk material but built on just one aspect of it: nasal timbre. I used mainly Eastern European, and particularly Rumanian folk music, and further developed its nasal character on tape. That, with some "live" vocal interventions is what provides the musical framework within which something else has to happen, and this "something else" can change from performance to performance. I can give you an example: some years ago, we performed it in Rome with Cathy Berberian, several folk singers, the Swingle Singers, a symphony orchestra that played a work by Pousseur and a speaker, who was, by the way, Umberto Eco. In Florence with the same framework, I used Monteverdi instead of Pousseur, different singers with a different repertoire, and a speaker who was saying something different.

As in certain sections of *Coro*, I used folk models which have one feature in common: the nasalization of the vocal technique. I developed this further on an electronic tape that I prepared at Bell Telephone Laboratories. The tape is a frame, a box, that can open here and there to let things in. I can put any foreign object in those openings or "windows" – Beethoven, Mozart, whatever you like. The frame closes, then it opens again – or else it can be left closed for a long time.

V: And what do the singers perform?

B: Partly music written by me, and partly quotations from folk music, with examples not only from Eastern Europe but also from Brittany, such as the *Chanson de Renaud*. That very old and very beautiful song was also used by Monteverdi as a tenor in the *Vespro della beata Vergine*. That is why in *Questo vuol dire che* my version is followed by his. Then Eastern Europe takes over once again. Like *Coro*, it is also a kind of a feast of songs, here linked by the electronic tape which ensures the unity of the whole. In the Roman performance, we had not only a symphony orchestra but acrobats and jugglers as well; in France we had chamber music; in Belgium we had Pousseur both as speaker and composer; at Carnegie Hall we had the President of Sarah Lawrence College, and so on.

V: It is a sort of musical happening.

B: Yes, but as a result of the constantly recurring folk elements it is a strictly organized happening.

INTERVIEW 2

with Bálint András Varga

V: If we may now pass on to your theatrical works, might I ask whether you have been inspired by a great personality, such as Beckett or Ionesco, in the development of your views on the theatre?

B: I am interested in all aspects of theatre. I grew up with Brecht, Pirandello, Shakespeare and Beckett. When I was fourteen or fifteen, I admired Ibsen even though I could hardly have understood him at that age. I even wrote an Ibsenian drama – it was of course a childish attempt.

V: A while ago, we mentioned Edoardo Sanguineti in passing. He wrote the texts for two of your stage works, Passaggio *and* Laborintus II.

B: We met in 1962 and it was "love" at first sight. Over the years we have given each other a lot. For me, poetry very often means Sanguineti, and for him, as he often says, music is Berio. On that level of identity, we can no longer speak of influence but of exchange of ideas.

Sanguineti is not only an outstanding poet whose art has many faces, but he is also an important Dante scholar. The text of *Laborintus* is such an organic unity that one can no longer tell what was written by Dante and what comes from Sanguineti. He is a scholar of enormous learning, a professor of Italian literature whose roots reach incredibly deep into the past.

When we worked on the texts of *Passaggio* and *Laborintus II* we conducted a continuous dialogue until the text was completed.

V: You said of Passaggio *that it was an anti-opera.*

B: *Passaggio* is an opera in the sense that it can only be performed in an opera house; it needs that medium, that frame. Its subject is the opera house itself. But I don't really think it can be called an anti-opera. To be correctly understood, it must imply the experience of opera.

The piece has a single character, the Woman. I also use two choruses. One is in the orchestra pit, the other one is in the hall, among the audience. In the course of performance, the Woman walks slowly from the back of the stage to the front and at the very end she addresses the audience.

V: She says: "Go away!"

B: Yes, it is quoted from Jean Genet's play, *Le Balcon*, which is set in a brothel where people put on disguises so as to be able to play out, with the prostitutes, roles that they cannot play in real life. Actually, it is a spectacle of degradation, especially that of powerful people, such as the bishop, the police chief and others. At the end, Irma, the owner of the brothel, on hearing that the revolution is getting nearer in the street, switches off the light and tells her clients: Go away, go to your home, which is even more false than this place.

V: I presume Genet's play is only referred to in this last episode. The lonely Woman on stage gets into different dramatic situations – she is arrested, tortured, sold and so on. Chorus A in the pit protects her, while chorus B is supposed to represent audience reaction. But do you seriously think that there are people in the stalls who would like to shout the kind of things that the chorus bellows on its behalf?

B: Subconsciously they must entertain such ideas. These are fascist reactions which are always present, unfortunately. It is no longer a question of audience but an aggressive mass which is against the freedom of the individual.

I shall never forget the premiere at the Piccola Scala. I conducted. I know that the audience would lose its head and had prepared the chorus, the Zurich Kammersprechchor for such an eventuality. I told them that once the audience began to shout, they should join in, take up the last word they heard and improvise on it. And that is precisely what happened. Some people shouted "Buffoni!" whereupon the chorus took it over, speeded it up, whispered it, lengthened the "o", and eventually the improvisation became part of the performance. The audience became hysterical because it had lost even the chance of protest. If someone began to whistle, twenty people would continue it. But later performances went off without any scandal – they even scored a considerable success.

V: And as for the music of Passaggio *is concerned?*

B: As the title indicates, the Woman passes from one dramatic situation into another, and meanwhile there is a passage from noise to music, from speech to singing, from instrumental to vocal music, from instrumental solo to tutti, from stage to audience – everything is in a constant state of flux. The same happens in the smaller units of the music. The part of the Woman is very difficult and requires great virtuosity. Every episode is very intense and demands a wide range of expression from the soloist – she reacts differently when she is found by unknown people (perhaps the Gestapo), when she is being questioned, when she is imprisoned, "sold", left alone and finally when she addresses the audience.

Laborintus II, on the other hand, does not necessarily demand a stage. Its musical material makes it suited to different forms of performance: as a concert piece, a documentary, a pantomime, etc. It uses different types of vocal technique: I wrote it for amateur singers, pop performers, actors who have not got a very cultivated singing voice.

When we performed *Laborintus* at La Scala, Sanguineti himself produced it. Maybe that was a mistake. I have nothing against genitals, but I did not like the spectacle of giant plastic phalluses slowly erecting on stage.

V: At one point in the score there is the instruction, "tempo jazz".

B: Yes, for the percussion players. With *Laborintus* I came closest to using a jazz orchestra: one flute, three clarinets, three trumpets, three trombones and two jazz drummers.

V: You also make it possible for musicians to improvise in free jazz style if they feel at home with it.

B: Yes, there is a tape in *Laborintus* that I prepared in Paris, with excellent jazz musicians. Good orchestral players, especially the double-bass, the trombone and the clarinet, can easily join in. There is only a short moment in the piece where this can happen, where the singers sing about *usura*, that is, the degradation of values. Otherwise, the tape was made largely in the Studio di Fonologia at the RAI in Milan and at Columbia University. The tape extends, transforms and develops certain vocal and instrumental aspects of the score. There is a very close tie between the tape and the live performance.

V: There is a longer passage where the soloists have nothing to do and we can only hear the orchestra and the tape. I suppose the accent here is on spectacle, for musically this section appears to have little interest.

B: That is where instruments and tape first come into contact without the singers.

V: Elsewhere there is an interesting dialogue between the singers and the instruments.

B: Yes, at times I emphasize the relationship between the voices and the instruments. At the beginning of the piece, for instance, the clarinet and the second trombone each take a note from a singer and develop it, and in doing so they play a fast passage as if imitating the singer. At another point the soloists and the eight actors imitate the cello, the double-bass and the trombone. Or a soprano mimics the cello, and the flute the soprano. By the time the message reaches the flute, it has become distorted. All that is simple enough musically to be tackled successfully by non-professional musicians: they must simply be able to listen and, of course, be very musical.

V: Our next subject is Opera. *All I know about it is what I read in a review of the Santa Fé première. Apparently it was not a success.*

B: It was one of the biggest disasters in my life. I wrote *Opera* for a fantastic ensemble, Open Theater from New York, which at that time was led by Jo Chakin. He is the only theatre producer respected even by Peter Brook.

I worked at the piece in a very difficult period of my life and perhaps I could not realize it on the level I had meant to. However, Chakin fell ill and could not undertake the direction of the Santa Fé première and things did not go well. One of the reasons why critics did not appreciate and understand it, however, was that they could not fit it in any of the known categories of the genre. Anyway, in recent years it has been performed to understanding audiences in Florence, Paris and Rome.

The title *Opera* is the plural of the word *opus*, and means works. It also means in this instance different techniques, different forms of stage behaviour.

Ideally, it ought to be performed on an empty, white stage which is filled by the actors with their presence – talking, dancing, singing, suggesting to the audience what is not there.

Opera is a highly complex piece – in fact, it is three works in one. The title therefore also refers to the three layers of meaning. One is Alessandro Striggio's *Orfeo*, set by Monteverdi, the second a production by Open Theater, *Terminal*, which centered on the terminal ward of hospitals where the dying are put, and the third is a modern myth, the sinking of the Titanic. In other words, all three have one subject in common: death. *Opera* is a celebration of ending.

V: Is it pessimistic?

B: Yes and no. There are many parodistic, grotesque elements in it – there is also a measure of detachment in a Brechtian sense. In a way, it is a "morality play". I have woven these three myths together with many subtle allusions. You cannot see the Titanic, Orpheus and Euridice; you cannot see – you shouldn't see dying people on the stage. The three myths fluctuate all the time, with motifs appearing and vanishing. This is where the difficulty of *Opera* lies and why it requires virtuoso performers. Only at the end is there a change of tone: suddenly everything darkens into tragedy as a new form of ending appears: the death of children.

That is how I stop the alternation of the three myths and show a different ending where there is no longer room for parody, grotesquerie and metaphor. There is no question of detachment any more, no indifference towards death – this is a real *fermata* . . .

Opera consists of lengthy episodes rather than acts. At the beginning, a soprano is learning an aria with the help of a pianist – the text is from the first act of Monteverdi's *Orfeo*. At other points of *Opera,* the soprano appears again, first singing a more accomplished version of the aria with piano accompaniment, then finally with an orchestra. This motif symbolizes growth and learning as do many other elements in the score which first make a sketchy appearance and then assume greater and greater significance. The structure of the music, the expressive nature of certain elements continue to grow while everything on stage is dying. This contrary motion is one of the basic elements of *Opera,* but the sudden change, the death of the children, puts an end to it. The growth of the music continues however, and tension increases as well, while fewer and fewer instruments are involved.

Opera ends with *Agnus* and *E Vo.* The children are dead, their bodies are lying on stage when *Agnus* is being played. Then a woman appears who approaches very very slowly, and when she finds a doll among the bodies of the dead children, she takes it in her arms and sings a lullaby. This is *E Vo.* That is where *Opera* ends and the lights slowly go out. In Sicily, women make their children sleep by singing "*e vó, e vó*" to them. The text of the little song is very beautiful and very simple. Come sleep, from your distant path and make him sleep! Sleep is obviously Death.

V: Certain numbers of Opera, *such as the soprano's aria* Air, *the tenor's* Melodrama, Agnus *and* E Vo *can be performed on their own. Can one draw the conclusion that the music of* Opera *is episodic in character?*

B: No. These numbers represent in reality the different stages of a continuous development. Certain elements are in constant motion – they appear, are transformed, disappear. The solution in *Sinfonia,* where the first movement only really ends in the last, occurs in *Opera* again and again. For instance, the second episode is a musically highly complex concerto where all the characters introduce themselves, as it were: they give their names, they tell what happened to them while the Titanic was sinking. The episode continues at the end of the piece, before the scene of the children: we can hear a development of the concerto and of the characters.

As for *Melodrama*, it is performed by a passenger from the Titanic. The idea was taken from my own experience. In the Fifties I often used to take a ship from Genoa to New York. The captain somehow always knew that I was a musician and asked me if I felt like performing something for the passengers. When Cathy was with me, we always used to sing and play on board. The tenor in *Opera*, who incidentally cannot sing, represents among other things a parody of such a situation.

V: And why Melodrama?

B: It is a parody of 19th century melodramas when recitation of poetry was accompanied by a few instruments. Nothing happens in it, the music is static – however fast and virtuosic the parts may be, the music does not move. And the tenor cannot sing the high *g*. But a discussion of *Opera* would need a book by itself . . .

V: You have also written a different kind of stage music: ballets. I am thinking of your early Allez-hop, *or the tape music composed for Béjart.*

B: My first ballet music was *Mimusic No 2* which was later adapted to a scenario by Calvino, and became *Allez-hop*. The ballet for Béjart was inspired by Petrarch's *Trionfi*. Its title is *Per la dolce memoria di quel giorno*. I wrote the orchestral score for it (and it lasts over an hour) within 15-20 days in a New York hotel. I shall never forget it.

V: Were you at all influenced in composing the ballet by the idea that your music would be danced to?

B: Only in very general terms. I was more influenced by Petrarch's *Trionfi* than by discussing the project with Béjart. I think, anyway, that the musician and the choreographer must keep a certain autonomy, even a certain indifference towards each other. But I wrote another dance piece, *Linea* for Felix Blaska, where I suggested the choreography myself.

V: Does the hour of music that you composed for Béjart stand on its own as a concert piece as well?

B: Only parts of it. As a matter of fact, I invested a great deal in that piece: it is built upon a tenor by Machault. Its organization is very strict at times and builds up to large structures. I had to work very fast and sometimes I wrote some of the orchestral parts separately – they were recorded and then the newly finished parts were superimposed and mixed together on tape. The rythmical aspects of Machault's tenor should maybe have been developed more.

V: Could I end with a more general question. In the third movement of Sinfonia, *the first tenor cries out that music cannot stop war, cannot make the old younger, nor lower the price of bread. You refer to the same theme in one of your articles. I assume you mean by this that music has no practical use. Yet at the same time you are very much aware of the composer's responsibilities. Isn't there a contradiction here? After all, what is music for? You asked that question yourself in an episode of* C'è musica e musica.

B: Yes, but there is no answer. If we knew it, we would stop writing music. If we could give a logical, practical, rational answer, music would be like functional speech where "signifier" and "signified" are ready-made.

V: But I think there is an answer. I remember attending two of Elisabeth Schwarzkopf's Lieder recitals. On both occasions I felt as if the blood was circulating faster in my veins and for days afterwards I felt a different person. I understood then that it was no empty phrase that music can make you better. And if music has that power, it does possess an important function.

B: Well, maybe that shows that you are a sensitive person and that you are not indifferent to some of the emotions of music. But I don't believe that music can make anybody better. Better for what? The Nazi officers playing string quartets were no better than the people entering the gas chamber next door; people absorbed in the music of Wagner and Beethoven are no better than people enjoying a pop song. As for my *Sinfonia*, when the tenor says that music cannot stop wars or lower the price of bread, he is making an indirect reference to Bertolt Brecht's *Badener Lehrstück*, the didactic play with music by Hindemith that he wrote as a comment on his previous *Lindbergh Flug*. After the difficult and courageous crossing of the ocean somebody says (I am quoting by memory): "we have built new machines, we have discovered a new continent where big places have been built - but the price of bread didn't go down". I would say that there is a typical dialectical opposition between the heroic crossing of the ocean and the price of bread as there is between a romantic Lieder cycle beautifully sung and your blood circulation. The meeting point among these dimensions is not the ocean nor the baker, is not German Romanticism nor your feeling better: it is always somewhere else. If music could lower the price of bread we wouldn't need it any more. Nevertheless, since we live and die in a world where people buy bread, cross oceans, make wars and music, we must continue asking ourselves questions about music and the price of bread ... I think that in music, the constant search for an answer to something that continuously shifts, the search for a deep unity, is maybe the most exciting, the most profoundly experimental and the least functional aspect of its presence. This is why sometimes we can receive, and we can also give music to others as a miraculous gift. The gift of becoming aware of questions that can be answered with other questions.

LUCIANO BERIO: A SHORT BIOGRAPHY

1925   Born on October 24 in Oneglia, a small town near Imperia on the Ligurian coast, into a family of local musicians: his father, in particular, attends to his early musical education.

1946-51   Pursues courses at the Milan Conservatory, while maintaining himself by a variety of musical activities. His principal teachers are Paribeni and Ghedini. Makes his first extensive contacts with the music of the twentieth century: particularly the second Viennese school, Bartok, Stravinsky, Hindemith and Milhaud.

1950   Marries the Armenian-American singer, Cathy Berberian, then studying in Milan. With her, he makes his first trip to the U.S.A.

1952   A bursary from the Koussevitzky Foundation enables him to return to the U.S.A. He studies with Dallapiccola at the Berkshire Music Festival in Tanglewood, Massachusetts, and hears tape music for the first time at a concert given in the Museum of Modern Art, New York.

1953   Birth of his first daughter, Cristina. He begins working for Italian television and radio – the RAI – in Milan. First encounters with Maderna and Pousseur.

1954   Attends the Darmstadt summer school for the first time – an association that he is to maintain sporadically for the next five years.

1955   After two years of experiment and persuasion, the *"Studio di fonologia musicale"* for electronic music is officially established at the RAI in Milan, directed by Berio in collaboration with Maderna.

1956   Berio and Maderna extend their entrepreneurial

activities by organizing the annual concert series, *"Incontri musicali"*, primarily devoted to contemporary music. Berio edits a journal of the same name, of which four numbers appear between 1956 and 1960.

1960   Resigns his post at the *Studio di fonologia,* and returns to the Berkshire School of Music in Tanglewood to teach composition – the first step in a progressive gravitation towards the U.S.A. as the centre of his activities.

1961-2 Teaches composition at the Dartington Summer School, England.

1962   Teaches the autumn semester at Mills College, Oakland, California.

1963-64 Returns to Mills College as Professor of Composition.

1965   Marries the Japanese psychologist, Susan Oyama. He transfers his activities to the East Coast, where he takes up teaching posts at both Harvard University and the Juilliard School of Music in New York.

1966   His second daughter, Marina, is born in Boston. He resigns his post at Harvard in order to concentrate on his work at the Juilliard School.

1967   Founds the Juilliard Ensemble, devoted to the performance of contemporary music.

1968   His first son, Stefano, is born in Hoboken, New Jersey.

1971   Resigns his post at the Juilliard School. He begins work, in Rome, on the television series *C'è musica e musica.*

1972   Definitively transfers the focus of his activities back to Italy. He buys the farmhouse below Radicondoli, in the Tuscan hills near Siena, which he gradually restores and finally, from 1975 on, moves into as his permanent Italian home.

1974	Accepts Boulez's invitation to direct the electro-acoustic section of the *Institut de Recherche et Coordination Acoustique Musique* (IRCAM) in Paris.
1975	Artistic Director of the Israel Chamber Orchestra.
1976	Artistic Director of the Accademia Filarmonica Romana.
1977	Marries the Israeli musicologist, Talia Packer.
1978	Birth of his second son, Daniel, in Paris.
1980	Resigns his post at IRCAM. Birth of his third son, Jonathan, in Paris. He accepts an honorary D. Mus. from City University, London.
1982	Artistic Director of the Orchestra Regionale Toscana.
1984	Artistic Director of the Maggio Musicale Fiorentino.

LUCIANO BERIO: A LIST OF WORKS

Compiled by David Osmond-Smith

There are several important sources that set out lists of Berio's work – most notably Mario Bortolotto's *Fase seconda*, Einaudi, Turin, 1969, David Collins' catalogue in *Musique en jeu*, 15, du Seuil, Paris, 1974, Claudio Annibaldi's entry on Berio in *The New Grove Dictionary of Music and Musicians*, ed. Stanley Sadie, Macmillan, London, 1980, and *Contrechamps 1*, ed. Philippe Albèra, L'Age d'Homme, Lausanne, 1983. There are unfortunately many discrepancies between them, particularly with regard to details of first performances. Where possible, I have attempted to disentangle these in consultation with the composer, but a number of uncertainties remain. This list must therefore be regarded as provisional.

Berio's two principal publishers, Suvini Zerboni and Universal Edition, are abbreviated throughout as S.Z. and U.E. respectively. Since from *Nones* on, saxophones are a normal part of Berio's woodwind section, I have included them in the numerical description of orchestration between clarinets and bassoons.

1937	*Pastorale* for piano
1939	Toccata for piano duet
1944	*Preludio a una festa marina* for string orchestra
1945-46	*L'Annunciazione* (Rilke) for soprano and chamber orchestra
1946	*Due cori popolari* for unaccompanied choir *Tre liriche greche* for voice and piano *O bone Jesu* for choir
1946-47	*Tre canzoni popolari* for voice and piano
1947	*Tre pezzi* for three clarinets

Petite Suite pour piano. U.E. 1st perf: Como, 1948

1948   *Quintetto* for wind
     Trio for strings
     Ad Hermes for voice and piano. 1st perf: Oneglia, 1948.
     E di te nel tempo for voice and piano
     Suite for piano. 1st perf: Como, 1948

1949   *Due pezzi sacri* for two sopranos, piano, two harps, timps and twelve bells
     Magnificat for two sopranos, chorus (SSAATB) and orchestra (1.1.2.0.0.–2.2.2.0., timps, percussion, vibraphone, two pianos, double bass). Belwin-Mills.
     1st perf: Turin, 1971, Berberian, Ross, Juilliard Ensemble, cond.Berio
     Concertino for solo clarinet, solo violin, harp, celesta and strings.U.E. 1st perf: Milan, 1950

1950   *Quartetto* for wind
     Tre vocalizzi for voice and piano
     El mar la mar (Alberti) for two sopranos, flute, clarinet, guitar, accordeon and double bass. Reduction for two sopranos and piano, 1953. Arranged for soprano, mezzo-soprano, flute (piccolo), two clarinets (bass clarinet), harp, accordeon, cello, double bass, 1969. U.E. 1st perf: Royan, 1969, Berberian, Rist

1950-51 *Opus No.Zoo* (Levine) for reciter and wind quintet. U.E. Revised 1971, with text recited by instrumentalists

1947-51 *Due liriche di Garcia Lorca* for bass and orchestra

1951   *Deus meus* for voice and three instruments. 1st perf: Milan, 1952, Berberian, Rensa, Abbado, Bergonzi
     Sonatina for wind quartet
     Due pezzi for violin and piano. S.Z. 1st perf: Tanglewood, 1952, Maazel, Lipkin

1952   *Study* for string quartet. 1st perf: Tanglewood, 1952

Adds to the *Tre canzoni popolari* of 1946-7 a fourth setting, "Dolce cominciamento", to form *Quattro canzoni popolari* for voice and piano. Revised 1973 U.E. 1st perf: Milan, 1952

1952-53   *Cinque variazioni* for piano. S.Z. 1st perf: Milan, 1953, Berio. Revised 1966

1953   *Mimusique No.1* for single track tape
Chamber Music (Joyce) for female voice, cello, clarinet and harp. S.Z. 1st perf: Milan, 1953, Berberian

1954   *Ritratto di città* for single track tape. Composed in collaboration with Bruno Maderna
Nones for orchestra (3.2.2.1.3.-4.4.3.1., timps, three percussionists, celesta, glockenspiel, vibraphone, xylophone, electric guitar, harp, piano, strings). S.Z. 1st perf: RAI, Turin, 1954, cond.Maderna
Variazioni for chamber orchestra (2.1.2.0.2.-2.2.1.0., strings). S.Z. 1st perf: NDR Hamburg, 1955, cond. Sanzogno

1955   *Mutazioni* for one-track tape. 1st perf: Milan, 1955
Mimusique No.2, mime piece on a scenario by Leydi, (3.2.3.0.3.-4.4.3.0., timps, percussion, glockenspiel, harp, celesta). S.Z 1st perf: Bergamo, 1955, cond. Maderna
Quartetto for strings. S.Z. 1st. perf: Darmstadt, 1955, Drolc Quartet
Allelujah I for five instrumental groups (I: four flutes, two oboes, two clarinets, bass clarinet, eight celli; II: E*b*, clarinet two saxophones, two bassoons, contra, six double basses; III celesta, vibraphone, marimba, xylophone, two harps, piano, glockenspiel; IV: four horns five trumpets, percussion, bells; V: four horns, three trombones, tuba, timps). 1st perf: WDR Cologne, 1956, cond. Gielen. Substantially reworked to form *Allelujah II* (see below)

1956   *Variazioni "ein Mädchen oder Weibchen"* for two basset horns and strings. Schott/U.E. 1st perf: Donaueschingen, 1956

1957   *Perspectives* for two-track tape. S.Z. 1st perf: Milan, 1957
Divertimento for orchestra (3.3.4.5.3.,-2.5.3.1., timps, four percussionists, celesta, glockenspiel, harp, piano, vibraphone, marimbaphone, xylophone, electric guitar, strings). 1st movement, "Dark rapture crawl", by Maderna; 2nd and 3rd movements, "Scat Rag" and "Rhumba-Ramble" by Berio. S.Z. 1st perf: RAI, Rome, 1957 cond. Maderna
Seranata for flute and fourteen instruments (0.1.cor anglais 2.0.1.-1.1.1.0., harp, piano, solo strings. S.Z. 1st perf: Paris, 1957, Gazzelloni, cond. Boulez

1957-58 *Allelujah II* for five instrumental groups (I: celesta, vibraphone, marimbaphone, electric guitar, two harps, piano, percussion, six double basses; II: four flutes, two clarinets, bass clarinet, two alto saxophones, timps, xylophone, percussion, four celli; III: four horns, three trombones, tuba, percussion, ten violins; IV: two oboes, cor anglais, E♭ clarinet, two bassoons, contra, three trumpets, percussion, glockenspiel, four celli; V: two tenor saxophones, four horns, three trumpets, two trombones, tuba, percussion, ten violas). S.Z. 1st performance, RAI Rome, 1958, cond. Maderna and Berio

1958   *Thema (Omaggio a Joyce)* for two-track tape. S.Z. 1st perf: Naples, 1958
Sequenza for flute. S.Z. 1st perf: Darmstadt, 1958, Gazzelloni

1958-59 *Tempi Concertati* for flute, violin, two pianos and instrumentalists (1.2.3.0 1 -1.1.1.0., percussion, two harps, two violas, two cellos, double bass) U.E. 1st perf: NDR, Hamburg, 1959, cond. Bour

1959   *Différences* for flute, clarinet, harp, viola, cello and tape. U.E. 1st perf: Paris, 1959 cond. Boulez

1952-59   *Allez Hop, "racconto mimico"* (mimed story) on a scenario by Calvino, for mimes and orchestra (3.3.4.4.3.-4.4.3.1., timps, harp, piano, celesta, glockenspiel, vibraphone, marimbaphone, electric guitar, four percussionists, strings). S.Z. 1st perf: Venice, 1959, cond. Sanzogno. Revised 1968. 1st perf: Bologna, 1968. Incorporates materials from *Mimusique No.2*

1959   *Quaderni I* for orchestra (4.4.4.0.4.-6.4.4.1., percussion, two harps, celesta, xylophone, glockenspiel, marimbaphone, vibraphone, strings). U.E. 1st perf: Donauschingen, 1959, cond. Rosbaud

1960   *Momenti* for four-track tape. U.E. 1st perf: Hamburg, 1960

1960   *Circles* (cummings) for female voice, harp and two percussionists. U.E. 1st perf: Tanglewood, 1960, Berberian

1959-61   *Epifanie* (Proust, Joyce, Machado, Simon, Brecht, Sanguineti) for female voice and orchestra (as in *Quaderni I*). U.E. 1st performance: Donaueschingen, 1961, cond. Rosbaud. Incorporates *Quaderni 1-3*. Revised 1965

1961   *Quaderni II* for orchestra (as in *Quaderni I*). U.E. 1st performance Vienna, 1961, cond. Rosbaud
           Visage for two track tape, using the voice of Cathy Berberian. 1st perf: RAI, Milan, 1961

1961-62   *Quaderni III* for orchestra (as in *Quaderni I*). U.E. 1st perf: Los Angeles, 1963, cond. Mehta

1962   *Passaggio* (Sanguineti) *"messa in scena"* (theatre piece) for soprano, Chorus A (in the pit), Chorus B (of five groups of speakers in the auditorium) and orchestra (2.0.2.2.2.,-1.2.2.1., harp, harmonium, electric guitar, five percussion groups, viola, cello and double bass). U.E. 1st perf: Milan, 1963, cond.Berio

1963   *Esposizione* (Sanguineti) for voices and instruments. 1st perf: Venice, 1963. Withdrawn and reworked to form part of *Laborintus II* (see below)
Sequenza II for harp. U.E. 1st perf: Darmstadt, 1963, Pierre
Traces (Oyama) for soprano and mezzosoprano solos, two actors, chorus and orchestra (2.0.3.3.1.-1.3.3.1., three percussionists, harp, lower strings. 1st perf: Iowa University, Iowa 1967. Withdrawn by Berio: some of the materials were reworked to be included in *Opera*

1964   *Sincronie* for string quartet. U.E. 1st perf: Grinnell, Iowa, Lenox Quartet, 1965
Folk Songs for mezzosoprano and seven instruments (flute, clarinet, 2 percussionists, harp, viola, cello). U.E. 1st perf: Oakland, California, 1964, Berberian. Arranged for mezzosoprano and orchestra (2.1.2 (plus bass clarinet) 0.1.-1.1.1.0., percussion, harp, strings). U.E. 1st perf: Zurich, 1973, Berberian, cond.Berio
Chemins I on *Sequenza II* for harp and orchestra (3.3.3.0.3.-4.3.3.1. two harps, celesta, harpsichord, piano, strings). U.E. 1st perf: Donaueschingen, 1965, Pierre

1965   *Wasserklavier* for piano. U.E. 1st performance: Brescia, 1970, Ballista
Laborintus II (Sanguineti) for three female voice, eight actors, one speaker and instruments (flute, three clarinets with bass clarinets, three trumpets, three

trombones, percussion, two harps, two cellos, two double basses. U.E. 1st perf: Paris, 1965, cond.Berio

Rounds for harpsichord. U.E. 1st perf: Basel, 1965, Vischer. Version for piano, 1967. U.E. 1st perf: 1968, New York, Spiegelmann

1965-66   *Sequenza III* for voice. U.E. 1st perf: Bremen, 1966, Berberian

Sequenza IV for piano. U.E. 1st perf: Saint Louis, 1966, de Carvalho

1966   *Gesti* for recorder. U.E. 1st perf: Amsterdam, 1967, Brueggen

Sequenza V for trombone. U.E. 1st perf: San Francisco, 1966, Dempster

1967   *Sequenza VI* for viola. U.E. 1st perf: New York, 1967, Trampler

Chemins II on *Sequenza VI* for viola and nine instruments (flute, clarinet, trombone, 2 percussionists, harp, electric organ, viola, cello). U.E. 1st perf: New York, 1967, Trampler

O King for mezzosoprano, flute, clarinet, piano, violin, viola, cello. U.E. 1st perf: Baldwin University, U.S.A., 1967, Aeolian Players. Incorporated into *Sinfonia* (see below)

1968   *Chemins III* on *Chemins II* for viola, nine instruments (as for *Chemins II*) and orchestra (3.0.3.3.0.3.-4.4.3.1., percussion, harp, celesta, strings). U.E. 1st perf: Paris, 1968, Trampler, cond.Berio

1968-69   *Sinfonia* for eight solo voices and orchestra (4.3.4.? 3 4.4.3.1., percussion, harp, piano, electric organ, electric harpsichord, strings). U.E. 1st perf: New York, 1968, Swingle Singers, Berio (first four movements only)

Questo vuol dire che for three female voices, small choir, tape, and other available resources. U.E. 1st perf: Rome, 1968, Eco, Berberian, Mantovani, Legrand, Swingle Singers

1969   *Sequenza VII* for oboe. U.E. 1st perf: Basel, 1969, Holliger
Chemins IIb for orchestra (2.1.1.2.2.-3.3.2.1., three percussionists, piano, electric organ, electric guitar, solo violin, six violas, four cellos, three double basses). U.E. 1st perf: Berlin, 1969, cond.Masson

1969-70   *Opera* (Berio, Eco, Colombo, Open Theater) for ten actors, soprano, tenor, baritone, vocal ensemble (SSAATTBB), orchestra (2.1.2.2.2.,-3.3.2.1., percussion, piano, electric organ, electric guitar, solo violin, six violas, four cellos, four double basses) and tape. U.E. 1st perf: Santa Fe, 1970, cond.Davies. Revised in 1977 to include *Agnus* and *E vo* (see below). Two other movements from *Opera* may be performed separately:
Air (Striggio) for soprano and orchestra (2.1.2.2.2.-3.0.0.0., percussion, vibraphone, marimbaphone, two pianos, electric organ, strings without double bass). U.E. 1st perf: Rovereto, 1971, Salvetta
Melodrama (Berio) for tenor and instruments (flute, clarinet, percussion, piano, electric organ, violin, cello, double bass). U.E. 1st perf: Siena, 1971

1970   *Erdenklavier* for piano. U.E. 1st perf: Bergamo, 1970, Ballista
Memory for electronic piano and harpsichord. U.E. 1st perf: New York, 1972. Revised 1973

1971   *Autre fois: berceuse canonique pour Igor Stravinsky,* for flute, clarinet and harp
Ora (Berio, Essam, after Virgil) for soprano, mezzo-soprano, flute, cor anglais, small choir and orchestra

(2.3.3.2.2.,-4.0.2.0. strings). 1st perf: Detroit, 1971 cond. Berio. Withdrawn

Bewegung for orchestra (3.2. plus cor anglais. 3.2.3.-4.4.3.1, percussion, harp, piano, electric organ, strings). U.E. 1st perf: Glasgow 1971, cond. Berio. *Bewegung II,* the same plus baritone, was subsequently withdrawn. *Bewegung* is currently undergoing revision. *Agnus* for two sopranos and three clarinetists. U.E. 1st perf: U.S.A. 1971

1972   *E vo* for soprano and instruments (1.1.3.0.0.-0.1.1.0. percussion, electronic organ, piano solo strings. U.E. 1st perf: Rovereto, 1972, Salvetta

Chemins IIC: Chemins IIB plus solo bass clarinet. U.E. 1st perf: Holland, 1972

Après Visage for tape and orchestra. 1st perf: Holland, 1972. Withdrawn

Recital for mezzosoprano and eighteen instruments (0.2.2.0.0.-2.1.1.0., percussion, harp, three pianos, solo strings). U.E. 1st performance: Lisbon, 1972, Berberian

1971-73   *Concerto* for two pianos and orchestra (2, piccolo. 2, cor anglais. 4.2.3. contra-3.3.3.1., electric organ, piano, marimbaphone,two percussionists, strings). U.E. 1st perf: New York, 1973, Canino, Ballista, cond. Boulez

1973   *Still* for orchestra (3.2, cor anglais. 4.2.3.-4.3.3.1., percussion, vibraphone, marimbaphone, harp, piano, electric organ, strings). U.E. 1st perf: Glasgow, 1973, cond.Gibson. Withdrawn

Cries of London for six voices. 1st perf: Edinburgh 1973, King's Singers. Revised 1975 for eight voices. U.E.

1973-74   *Eindrücke* for orchestra (as for *Still*) U.E. 1st perf: Zurich, 1974, cond. Leinsdorf

1974   *Calmo (in memoriam Bruno Maderna)* (Homer) for

soprano and instruments (1.1.2.0.1.-1.1.1.0., strings).
U.E. 1st perf: Milan, 1974
Points on the curve to find . . . . for piano and twenty-two
instruments (3.1, cor anglais. 3.2.2.-2.2.1.1., celesta,
viola, two cellos, double bass). U.E. 1st perf: Donan-
eschingen, 1974, Bonaventura, cond. Bour
Per la dolce memoria de quel giorno, ballet based on
Petrarch's *I trionfi* with choreography by Béjart, for
tape. U.E. 1st perf: Florence, 1974
*Musica Leggera, canone per moto contrario e al rovescio, con
un breve intermezzo* for flute and viola, accompanied by a
cello. Written to celebrate Petrassi's seventieth birthday

1974-75   *A-Ronne,* radio documentary for five actors on a poem
by Sanguineti. U.E. 1st perf: Hilversum Radio, 1974.
Concert version for eight voices, 1975. U.E. 1st perf:
Lièges, 1975, Swingle II
Chants parallèles for tape. U.E. 1st perf: ORTF,
France, 1975

1975   *Diario immaginario* radio piece (Sermonti, after
Molière's *Le malade imaginaire*) U.E. 1st perf: RAI,
Florence, 1975
Sequenza VIII for violin. U.E. 1st perf: Paris 1976,
Chiarappa
Fa-Si for organ. U.E.

1975-76   *Coro* for forty voices (10 S, 10 A, 10 T, 10 B) and
instruments (4.1, cor anglais. 4.2.3.-3.4.3.1., percussion, piano, electric organ, three violins, four
violas, four cellos, three double basses). U.E. 1st perf:
Donaueschingen, 1976 cond. Berio. Extended 1977

1977   *Il ritorno degli Snovidenia* for cello and thirty instruments (3.2.3.1.2.-2.2.2.1., piano, 3.3.3.2.) U.E. 1st
perf: Basel, 1977, Rostropovich, cond. Sacher

1978   *Les mots sont allés* for cello. U.E. 1st perf: Basel, 1978,
        Rostropovich
        Encore for orchestra (2 piccolos, 2.2, cor anglais. 4.1.2,
        contra – 3.3.3.1, timps, percussion, harp, celesta,
        piano, strings). U.E. 1st perf: Rotterdam, 1978, cond.
        Zillmann

1980   *Chemins V* for clarinet and digital system. U.E. 1st perf:
        Paris, 1980, Arrignon. Work in progress
        Sequenza IX for clarinet, drawn from *Chemins V*.
        U.E.
        Transcribed for saxophone as *Sequenza IX B*, 1981.
        U.E.

1977-81 *La Vera storia* (Calvino), opera in two acts for soprano,
        mezzosoprano, tenor, baritone, bass, vocal ensemble
        (SSAATTBB) and orchestra (4 plus two piccolos. 1
        plus cor anglais. 4.2.3.-3.3.3.1., timps, percussion,
        harp, two pianos, electronic organ, strings), U.E. 1st
        perf: Milan, 1982, Milcheva, Milva, Nicolescu,
        Schiavi, Di Credico, Luccardi, New Swingle Singers,
        Scaparo, cond. Berio. Materials from the opera were
        given separate performance before completion under
        the titles *Scena* (1st perf: Rome, 1979) and *Entrata* (1st
        perf: San Francisco, 1980, cond. de Waart). They
        have since been re-absorbed into the opera.

1980-81 *Accord* for four groups of wind instruments (2 piccolos
        2.1.3.3.-2.2.2. two each of soprano, alto, tenor and
        baritone flügelhorns 3. three bass tubas, percussion).
        U.E. 1st perf: Assisi, 1980
        Corale on *Sequenza VIII* for violin, two horns and
        strings. U.E. 1st perf: Zürich, 1982, Chiarappa

1982   *Duo* (Calvino) *"teatro immaginario"* for baritone, two
        violins, choir and orchestra (2.2.3.1.3.-3.3.3.1., strings)
        U.E. A study for *Un re in ascolto* (see below)

1983   *Lied* for clarinet. U.E. 1st perf: Geneva, 1983

1979-83   *34 duetti* for two violins. U.E.

1979-84   *Un re in ascolto* (Calvino, Berio), *"azione musicale"* in two acts. U.E. 1st perf: Salzburg, 1984, Adam, Armstrong, Greenberg, Kuhlmann, Sima, Helm, Lohner, Molcho, Moser, Muff, Tichy, Wildhaber, Zednik, cond. Maazel

1984   *Requies* for orchestra, U.E. 1st perf: Lausanne, 1984 cond. Jordan
         Voci for viola and instrumental ensemble. In preparation
         Sequenza X for trumpet. In preparation

ARRANGEMENTS

1966   *Monteverdi: Il combattimento di Tancredi e Clorinda* for soprano, tenor, baritone, three violas, cello, double bass and harpsichord. U.E. 1st perf: New York, 1966

1969   *The Modification and Instrumentation of a Famous Hornpipe as a Merry and Altogether Sincere Homage to Uncle Alfred Purcell,* arranged for flute or oboe, clarinet, percussion, harpsichord, viola, cello

1972   *Weill: Le grand lustucru* (from *Marie galante*), arranged for mezzosoprano and instruments (1 plus piccolo. 1.2.1. two trumpets, percussion, solo strings).U.E. Weill: *Surabaya Johnny* (from *Happy End*), arranged for mezzosoprano and instruments (flute, clarinet, trumpet, percussion, guitar, solo strings

1975   *Weill: Ballade von der Sexuellen Hörigkeit* (from *Die Dreigroschenoper*), arranged for mezzosoprano and instruments (clarinet, bass clarinet, vibraphone, accordeon, solo strings). U.E.
Quattro versioni originali della Ritirata notturna di Madrid di L.Boccherini sovrapposte e trascritte per orchestra (3.plus piccolo 2.plus cor anglais 3.0.3.-4.4.3.1., timps, percussion, harp, strings. U.E. 1st perf: Milan, 1975, cond. Bellugi

1978   *de Falla: Siete canciones populares espanolas* arranged for mezzosoprano and orchestra (2.1 plus cor anglais 3.0.2.-2.2.2.1., timps, castanettes, percussion, strings. U.E. 1st perf: Rochester, 1978, cond. Berio.

INDEX